Elementary

English for

BUSINESS LIFE

IAN BADGER   PETE MENZIES

Course Book

D1421795

Marshall Cavendish
Education

Acknowledgements

The authors would like to thank the following for their great help and advice in the preparation of *English for Business Life*: Simon Ross, Lucy Brodie, Jo Barker, Graham Hart and Teresa Miller.

We would also like to thank our business 'students' from organisations including UPM-Kymmene Oyj, Metso Paper, BEMIS, Peterson Packaging, Vattenfall, the International Maritime Organisation, GE Finance, ABN Amro (Investment Bank), Dresdner Kleinwort Wasserstein (UK), Matsushita Europe and Marketing Akademie Hamburg for providing the inspiration and feedback that underpins *English for Business Life*.

Finally, the authors would like to thank their families for their support and forbearance during the writing process! – Gerry, Ollie and Elly Badger; Helen Glavin for hours of research; Miranda Glavin for her invaluable input and support.

© Marshall Cavendish Ltd 2005

© Ian Badger & Pete Menzies 2005 (Text only)

First published 2005 by Marshall Cavendish Ltd

Marshall Cavendish is a member of the Times Publishing Group

Marshall Cavendish ELT
119 Wardour Street
London W1F 0UW

Designed by Hart McLeod, Cambridge

Printed and bound by Edelvives, Zaragoza, Spain

Photo acknowledgements

Pg.12 image100 / Alamy; Pg.15 t Comstock Images / Alamy, b Iconica; Pg.17 BananaStock / Alamy; Pg.18/19 Freefoto.com; Pg.20 l AceStockLimited / Alamy, r Rex; Pg.22 Iconica; Pg.24 Iconica; Pg.26 Iconica; Pg.29 Joseph Sohm; ChromoSohm Inc. / Corbis; Pg.31 The Photolibrary Wales / Alamy; Pg.32 Brand X Pictures / Alamy; Pg.33 Iconica; Pg.34 Iconica; Pg.35 BananaStock / Alamy; Pg.37 Rex; Pg.38 Imagestate; Pg.41 l LWA-Stephen Welstead/Corbis, r Comstock Images / Alamy; Pg.44 Peter Bowater / Alamy; Pg. 45 Image State / Alamy; Pg.47 Brand X Pictures / Alamy; Pg.48 ImageState / Alamy; Pg.50/51 Jon Bower / Alamy; Pg.54 Andrew Curran / Alamy; Pg.55 Photonica; Pg.57 Iconica; Pg.59 Photonica; Pg.60 Iconica; Pg.62 Philip Harvey / Corbis; Pg.63 Photonica; Pg.65 Photonica; Pg.66 FLPA / Alamy; Pg.69 James Leynse / Corbis; Pg.70 Royalty-Free / Corbis; Pg.72 Tom Wagner / Corbis Saba; Pg.75 SIE Productions / Corbis; Pg.77 Jackson Smith / Alamy; Pg.79 Iconica; Pg.80 Francis Li / Alamy; Pg.82 Brand X Pictures / Alamy; Pg.83 Rex; Pg.84 tl Tony Arruza / Corbis, cl Iconica, cr Robert Dowling / Corbis; Pg.86 Kim Karpeles / Alamy; Pg.88 l Image100 / Alamy, r Dynamic Graphics Group / Creatas / Alamy, cl Dynamic Graphics Group / Creatas / Alamy; Pg.89 Stock Connection / Alamy; Pg.90 Iconica; Pg.91 Jeff Greenberg / Alamy; Pg.92 Alex Serge / Alamy; Pg.94 David Crausby / Alamy; Pg.95 Rex; Pg.97 Photonica; Pg.98 Uppa; Pg.101 Garry Gay / Alamy; Pg.102 Royalty-Free / Corbis; Pg.104 Jeff Morgan / Alamy; Pg.106 t James Bartholomew / Alamy, b Adesse Images / Alamy; Pg.107 Andre Jenny / Alamy; Pg.108 Imagstate; Pg.110 Rex; Pg.113 G P Bowater / Alamy; Pg.116 Royalty-Free / Corbis; Pg.117 Amet Jean Pierre / Corbis Sygma; Pg. 118 Royalty-Free / Corbis; Pg.120 Royalty-Free / Corbis

Contents

Contents chart

UNIT	EXPRESSIONS	STUDY POINTS	FEATURES
1 About you	My name is … I am (I'm) from Berlin. I work for MAT. I am an engineer. My mobile number is 071568243.	*a/an* The verb *to be* (*am, is, are*) Subject pronouns (*I, you, he, she,* etc.) Titles (Mr, Mrs etc.) Numbers 1–9	Giving your (telephone) number
2 About your job	I work for an insurance company. Do you work in the sales department? I am (I'm) the Assistant Sales Manager. I like my job (it) very much.	The use of *the* The Simple Present tense Object pronouns (*me, him, her, it,* etc.)	Spelling names The alphabet
3 About where you work	I work in an office in the centre of town. It is (It's) near the station. There are some good restaurants nearby. My office is on the first floor.	*there is/are* *some/any* The verb *to have*	Giving an address Numbers: cardinal 1–100; ordinal 1st–10th
4 Your business activities	We make parts for computers. We are (We're) in the IT business. We do a lot of business in Western Europe. We're working on a new product. Business is going well.	*a lot of/much/many* The Present Continuous tense (*We're working* …) *make/do* (*make computers, do business,* etc.)	Parts of the world (Western Europe, etc.) Percentages (90% of our business)
5 The location of your company	Our engineers' offices are five kilometres west of the city. They are (They're) in Inchon. It is (It's) about 300 kilometres from Pusan. Where are your company's main offices?	Possessive adjectives (*my, your, his,* etc.) Possessive nouns (*the company's offices*) Plural nouns	Numbers 100–1000 Compass points (west of, to the south, etc.)
6 The layout of your company	This is the service department. Where is (Where's) the conference centre? It is (It's) behind the main block. Go down here. It's on the left.	Demonstrative adjectives (*this, these, those,* etc.) Imperatives (*Go/Don't go*) Prepositions of place (*behind, in front of,* etc.) Prepositions of direction (*to, down,* etc.)	Giving directions Signing in
7 Meeting and welcoming	I would (I'd) like to welcome you to KPG. How was your trip? It was fine. This is Bill Smith, our PR Manager. Pleased to meet you.	The Past tense of *to be* (*was, were*) *a little/a few*	Nationalities and languages (French, English, etc.) Introductions

UNIT	EXPRESSIONS	STUDY POINTS	FEATURES
8 The first two minutes	How are you? How is (How's) business? How do you like New York? How long are you here for? I hear you are (you're) leaving tomorrow.	The Present Continuous for the future (*I'm leaving tomorrow*.) *I hear, I see, I understand, I believe*	Days of the week (*Monday*, etc.) Parts of the day (*this morning, tomorrow afternoon*, etc.)
9 Partings and thanks	Call me next week. I will (I'll) call you next week. Give my regards to your wife. Thanks for everything. You are (You're) welcome.	Imperatives for requests (*Give my regards to …*) *will* for promises (*I'll call you*.) *must* for inviting (*You must visit us*.)	Months (*January, February*, etc.) Seasons (*spring, summer*, etc.) Festivals (*New Year, Independence Day*)
10 Setting up a meeting	Are you free tomorrow? Can you make Friday? I will (I'll) see you at four o'clock. I am (I'm) afraid I cannot (can't) make it.	*can/can't* Prepositions of time (*at four o'clock*)	Telling the time (*3.30, 4.20*, etc.) Saying the date (*the 26th of April*) Ordinal numbers 11th–100th
11 Confirming arrangements	I am (I'm) calling to confirm Tuesday's meeting. Are you still OK for Monday? Can I check the time? Do you know where it is (yet)?	*still/yet* Embedded/Indirect questions (*Do you know where it is?*) *to/in order to* (*I'm calling to …*)	Confirming a schedule am/pm
12 Changing plans	The conference room is booked. We will (We'll) have to start earlier. Can we change it to next week? Will the room be free by two o'clock?	*will/will not* *have to* *why* and *because*	Suggestions (*Why don't we …?* and *Let's …*)
13 Dealing with the unexpected	I am (I'm) calling to ask if we could postpone the meeting. There is a security alert. The airport is closed. I'm afraid I'm not going to make it. I'm sorry about this. Do not (don't) worry. I can't make it either.	*going to* (*going to be busy*) *could* in requests (*Could we call it off?*) Phrasal verbs (*call off/put off*) *too/either* (*I'm ill too*.)	Postponing/Cancelling
14 Explaining and apologising	I am (I'm) sorry I missed our appointment yesterday. I had to take my wife to the doctor. She has a cough. I wanted to phone, but I did not (didn't) have your number in my mobile.	The Past tense (regular and irregular verbs) *had to*	Some family members (*husband, wife*, etc.) Some common ailments (*cough, cold*, etc.) Apologies

UNIT	EXPRESSIONS	STUDY POINTS	FEATURES
15 Making contact by phone	Is it possible to speak to Pete Semler? Can I have extension 401 please? Is that Mr Semler? This is Ed Roza from BRAC.	*Is it possible to …?* *this/that* (in telephoning)	Telephone alphabets Spelling on the phone Email addresses
16 Dealing with incoming calls	Who is (Who's) calling, please? She is (She's) away from her desk at the moment. You are (You're) through to the wrong extension. I will (I'll) get him to call you.	*who* (*Who did you speak to?*) *for/until (till)*	Telling the time (*a quarter past, half past three*, etc.)
17 Leaving and taking messages	Can I leave a message? Can I take a message? Could you say that Mr Gitto called? Sorry, I did not (didn't) catch that.	*ask/say/tell* (*Could you ask him to …?*) Numbers (hundreds/thousands/ millions)	Messages Money (€8, $100, ¥5,000)
18 Email and telephone problems	I tried to call you at about nine. I could not (couldn't) get through. Your extension was on voicemail. My email bounced back. Can I check your address?	Approximate times (*at about …, just after …*) *try* + infinitive (*I tried to call you.*)	Some telephone and email vocabulary Email and web addresses
19 Drinks and snacks	Would you like a cup of coffee? Can I get you anything else? Whose coffee is this? I think this one is mine.	Possessive pronouns (*mine, yours*, etc.) *whose* (*Whose coffee is this?*) *one/ones* (*That's my one.*) *something/anything*	Tea and coffee vocabulary Snack vocabulary
20 Eating out	Do you like Mexican food? Can we have the menu please? What do you recommend? I will (I'll) have the chicken. The starter was better than the main course.	Comparative adjectives (*cheaper, more expensive*) *a piece of cake, a litre of beer*	Food and restaurant vocabulary More percentages (15%, 17½%, 45.5%)
21 Outings and sightseeing	Have you been to Barcelona before? Would you like to go for a drive round? This is the most interesting part of town. That is (That's) the oldest part of the factory.	The Present Perfect (*Have you been here before?*) Superlative adjectives (*biggest, most modern*) *since* (*I haven't been there since 2001.*) *for* (*I haven't seen him for five years.*)	Types of entertainment
22 Starting a journey	Is this the right check-in for Tokyo? Do I need to clear customs in Tokyo? How many bags do you have? Where is the platform for Avignon? Can I have a single to Milan?	*to need to* *How much? How many?*	PA announcements Checking in

UNIT	EXPRESSIONS	STUDY POINTS	FEATURES
23 Travelling	What time do we arrive in Hong Kong? We are (We're) due in at five. Is there a bus service to the centre of town? Have you got today's newspapers? Is this Madison Avenue?	The Simple Present (for the future) Possessive -'s (*today's newspapers*) *have got*	Periods of time (*in a quarter of an hour, in half an hour*) Timetables
24 Arriving and meeting contacts	Did you have a good journey? How was the weather in Lisbon? It was raining when I left. Shall we go through your programme?	The Past Continuous (*It was raining.*) *shall* for suggestions (*Shall we go through the programme?*)	Some weather vocabulary
25 Gifts and saying thank you	Thank you for showing us round. We enjoyed it very much. This is for you. Thank you. It is (It's) very kind of you.	*enjoy/like* + verb + *-ing* (*We enjoyed having you.*) *so/neither* (*So did I. Neither did I.*) *nor*	Parting Gifts
26 Checking facilities and information	Is there a scanner I can use? Is there a beamer we could use? Which one can I borrow? Could you print these handouts for me?	To do something for someone *Which?* (*Which one can I borrow?*) *borrow/lend*	Some office equipment
27 Shopping	How much are these T-shirts? They are (They're) €20 each. Have you got this in a bigger size? What is (What's) that in a continental size? Where can I find perfume?	*might/may* (*I might/may buy a new coat.*) Ages (*a six year-old child*)	Clothing sizes Payment (*Can I pay by credit card?*)
28 Your colleagues	Which one is your boss? He is (He's) the tall one with glasses. He has (He's) been with the company for ten years. I do not (don't) think he is married.	The Present Perfect tense (*He has been …*) *ago* (*She joined us three weeks ago.*)	Describing people (*He's tall with glasses.*) Some family details (*She has two children.*)
29 Your office building	I am (I'm) looking for the training department. It is (It's) at the end of the corridor, on the left. It's not far. I'm not sure where it is.	Prepositions of place (*above, at*, etc.) Prepositions of direction (*into, up to*, etc.) Indirect questions *How far? A long way. Not far.*	Giving directions in a building

UNIT	EXPRESSIONS	STUDY POINTS	FEATURES
30 How things work	Do you know how it works? First, plug it in. Then … You switch it on like this. Does it normally make that noise? I think there's a problem. I can't access my files.	Adverbs of frequency (*normally, usually*, etc.) Phrasal verbs (*switch on/off, turn on/off*) The Simple Passive (*It isn't plugged in.*)	Sequences (*First …, then …*)
31 Requesting information	Could I have some information on filing cabinets, please? Could you give me the catalogue number? It is (It's) available in blue or red. Do you have them in stock?	Measurements of length (1.25m, 90cm) Order of adjectives (*a large blue one*)	Some office furniture Imperial measurements (miles, feet, etc.) Confirming in writing
32 Staying in a hotel	I would (I'd) like to book a room, please. How many nights do you want the room for? It is (It's) just for tonight. I am (I'm) afraid we are (we're) full.	*How …! What a …!* (*How irritating! What a nuisance!*) *so/such* Reflexive pronouns (*myself, yourself*, etc.)	Booking a hotel room Room names (bedroom, dining room, etc.)
33 Booking conference facilities	We are (We're) looking for a room for a conference. I think Room A is too small. Room B is 25 metres long. When do you want it? All day.	Dimensions and measurements (*It's 25 metres long.*) *too* + adjective (*too small*) *not … enough* (*not big enough*)	Charges (€1,750 a day)
34 Organising a trip	I would (I'd) like a return ticket to Bahrain. I will (I'll) call you when the tickets are ready. The flight leaves at 09.15. You could go by train. It would be cheaper.	*when* + the Present tense (*I'll call you when they are ready.*) *would* (*It would take longer.*)	The 24-hour clock (*oh five fifteen*) Spelling/pronouncing (*How do you pronounce …?*)
35 Hiring a car	There is (There's) a car-hire place inside the airport. What size car do you want? It is (It's) $450 per week, including tax. That seems OK.	*seem/sound/look* (*That seems OK.*) *like* (*something like a Focus*) Comparisons (*like/not like*)	Car talk (make, year, colour, model, etc.) Forms (date of birth, date of issue, etc.) Rates/charges
36 Returning home	Welcome back. How was your trip? I needed more time in Lima. I managed to travel on Sunday instead. Dick sent you his regards.	*instead (of)* *more than/less than* *want* + object + infinitive (*They want me to …*) *I'm afraid so/not*	Changing bookings

Introduction

Business Life is a four-level course designed for people who need English for their everyday work. *Business Life* is:

- a course written by authors with a wide experience of teaching English for business in a range of international contexts, countries and cultures
- a course that respects the modern need for flexibility; learners can follow fast, standard or comprehensive tracks through the materials
- a course that follows a progressive and comprehensive grammar syllabus, with the stress on the effective use of grammar for clear communication
- a course that satisfies the requirements of the Common European Framework, BEC and equivalent global testing authorities
- a course that supports the learner in a highly connected modern world.

Each level of the course consists of:

- a course book with detachable answer booklet
- two CDs containing course book listening exercises
- a self-study guide packaged with an accompanying audio CD
- a trainer's manual.

Learners can follow fast, standard and comprehensive tracks through the material – 40 to 90 hours of work:

- fast track – 40 hours
- standard track – 60 hours
- comprehensive track – 90 hours.

Summary of components
Course book

The course book consists of:

- 36 units at Elementary and Pre-intermediate level (26 units at Intermediate and Upper intermediate levels)
- a glossary of business-related terms
- a grammar/language index
- a word list
- tapescripts of all listening activities
- answers in a detachable booklet.

Two audio CDs are available as a separate component.

Self-study guide

The Self-study guide consists of:

- 36 parallel units + progress tests (26 units at Intermediate and Upper Intermediate levels)
- material that can be used in support of the Course Book or as a self-standing resource
- audio CD containing recordings of core language, pronunciation points and listening exercises
- reinforcement/consolidation exercises
- a grammar/language reference section
- a glossary of business-related terms.

Trainer's manual

The trainer's manual consists of:

- notes on exercises and ideas for consolidation/extension work
- a glossary of business-related terms
- notes on business practice
- answers and tapescripts for course book exercises.

Business English exams/testing equivalence

Levels	Common European Framework Level	ALTE	BEC	London Chamber of Commerce (EFB)
Upper Intermediate	B2–C1	4	Higher	Fourth level
Intermediate	B1	3	Vantage	Third level
Pre-intermediate	A2–B1	2	Preliminary	Second level
Elementary	A2			Preliminary/ first level

Useful websites

For more on the European Framework visit www.ALTE.org
For BEC visit www.cambridgeesol.org/exams/bec.htm
For the 'Business Language Testing Service' visit www.BULATS.org
For the London Chamber of Commerce Exams visit www.lccieb.com
For the TOEIC American exams for working people visit www.ets.org/toeic

Who is *Business Life* for?

Business Life presents the language that is essential for doing business in English; it has strong global relevance. Groups that will benefit from using the materials include:

- business schools and colleges
- language schools which offer English for business courses
- company training courses and study programmes
- vocational adult education classes
- schools and colleges which aim to equip their students with the language skills they will need in their working lives.

What is the level of the Elementary book?

The Elementary level of *Business Life* is for 'false beginners'. You may have studied English for two or three years at school, or you may have picked up English in your work without studying it formally. You will therefore be able to manage English at a basic survival level, but will have difficulty if the topic of communication moves away from very familiar matter. You will need to revise the basic structures of the language, and you will probably want to build confidence in order to handle everyday business and social situations in English.

Alternatively, you may have a higher level of general English but need specifically to improve your English for business communication.

Content

The materials cover the full range of everyday business communications skills – speaking, listening, reading and writing. There is a wide variety of guided and free-practice exercises. The aim is to find out what learners can do in English within a given theme and then to help them to develop their skills.

Each unit also contains a number of study points – grammar and vocabulary. The grammar sections are concerned specifically with helping the learner to use the language accurately for effective and clear communication. There is a grammar/language index at the back of the course book.

There are additional language notes, exercises and progress tests in the Self-study workbook.

Flexibility: different tracks through the materials

Fast track: 40 hours (approximately 1 hour per unit) involving:

- introductory discussion on each theme
- study points
- listening – key dialogues
- practice activities.

Standard track: 60 hours (approximately 1¾ hours per unit) involving:

- introductory discussion on each theme
- reading
- study points
- listening – key dialogues
- practice activities
- study notes and exercises from the Self-study workbook as appropriate.

Comprehensive track: 90 hours (approximately 2½ hours per unit) involving:

- introductory discussion on each theme
- reading
- study points
- listening – key dialogues + additional listening exercises
- practice activities
- detailed study of related Self-study workbook materials.

Some study tips

- Make time for your English studies. Approach them with the same level of commitment that you would any other project in your work or spare time.
- Find the study pattern that works best for you. In our view 'little and often' is more effective than occasional long sessions.
- Keep an organised study file. Make sure that the language that is most relevant to your needs is clearly highlighted.
- Ensure that you relate the language presented in the course back to your area of business or study. If there are terms you need which are not included in the material, consult your trainer, English-speaking colleagues and friends, and make thorough notes.
- Make use of the English-speaking media – web pages, radio, TV, professional journals, magazines and newspapers to follow up your business and leisure interests in English.
- Make use of monolingual and bilingual dictionaries. A number of dictionaries are available on-line and the 'synonym' and 'thesaurus' keys on your computer are always useful.

Study Themes in *Business Life*

Elementary level

- You and your job
- Your company
- Brief exchanges
- Arrangements
- Telephoning
- Business hospitality
- Business trips
- Your working environment
- Enquiring and booking

Other levels

Pre-intermediate level

- You and your company
- Meeting people
- Time off
- The workplace
- Numbers and figures
- Business travel
- The product
- Arrangements
- Business entertaining
- Sales and selling
- Requesting/supplying information

Intermediate level

- Contacts
- Companies
- Personnel
- Products
- Services
- Entertaining
- Meetings
- Travel
- Money and finance
- Presentations

Upper intermediate level

- A company visit
- Company background
- Conditions of employment
- Travelling on business
- Money and finance
- Efficiency at work
- Sales and marketing
- Outside working hours
- Business and government
- Projects

The authors

IAN BADGER has extensive experience of developing courses and systems of language training for business. He is a partner in Business and Medical English Services, and a director of English4 Ltd. His publications include *Everyday Business English, Everyday Business Writing* (Longman) and *Business English Phrases* (Penguin).

PETE MENZIES is an associate of Pod (Professional and Organisational Development) and founder of Commnet, a dedicated training agency specialising in written communication and email management. Awards for his published work include the Duke of Edinburgh ESU Prize and the Gold Medal at the Leipzig Industrial Fair.

UNIT 1 About you

1 Key dialogues

Overview

Listen to the dialogues (a–d) and answer the questions.

a Is Jochen Gramm from MAT?
Where's Della Lorn from?

b Is it Mr Owen?
Who is it?

c Is Trevor Muller in Sales?
Where's Sally Gigot from?

d What's Ms Hagel's first name?
Is Miranda Murphy an engineer?

2 Study points

Check the Language Notes as you do these exercises.

a/an

1 Use *a* or *an* to fill in the gaps in these sentences.

a I'm .... engineer.

b It's .... interesting job.

c Are you .... sales rep?

d I work for .... multinational company.

e She is .... IT consultant.

f Is it .... American company?

g He isn't .... designer.

h It's .... French name.

Present tense of the verb to be

2 Fill in the gaps in the following sentences. Practise the dialogue with a partner.

A: **a** .... Susan Hogg from Finance?

B: No, **b** ....

A: Where **c** .... ? Do you know?

B: No, I don't. **d** .... in the office.

A: Does she have a mobile (phone)?

B: I think so.

A: What **e** .... her number?

B: **f** .... sorry. I don't know.

A: **g** .... from the finance department?

B: No, **h** .... **i** .... a receptionist.

Telephone numbers

3 Say these telephone numbers. Then, in pairs, practise giving your office and mobile numbers.

a 733 046 2100
b 257 08439
c 010628844
d 23 61 77
e 0655 5291
f 628 35092
g 744 290 011
h 363404815

Subject pronouns

4 In pairs, practise the subject pronouns by giving short answers. **Partner A** asks questions from the table. **Partner B** answers. Refer to the Language Notes for help.

Questions		**Answers**
Am I	[Bill Smith]?	Yes, I am.
Are you	a [sales rep]?	No, I'm not.
Is [John]	an [engineer]?	Yes, you are.
Is [Mary]	in the [sales] dept?	No, you aren't.
Is [your name/number]	[706 328]?	I don't know.
Are you and [John]	from [New York]?	
Are [John] and I	from [ICT]?	etc.
Are [John] and [Mary]	[accountants]?	

3 Guided practice

Making contact

In pairs, use the flowchart to practise saying who you are.

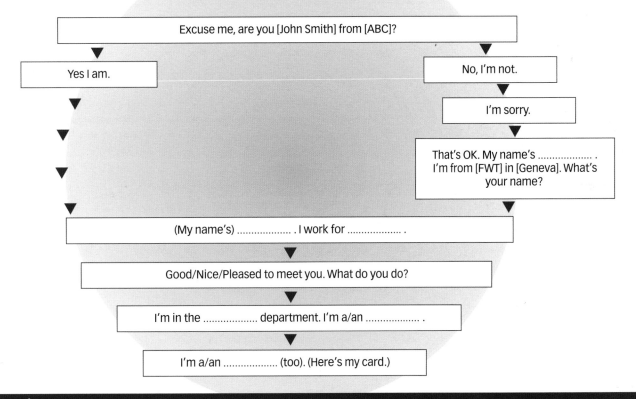

Excuse me, are you [John Smith] from [ABC]?

Yes I am.

No, I'm not.

I'm sorry.

That's OK. My name's .... I'm from [FWT] in [Geneva]. What's your name?

(My name's) .... I work for ....

Good/Nice/Pleased to meet you. What do you do?

I'm in the .... department. I'm a/an ....

I'm a/an .... (too). (Here's my card.)

4 Listening

Voice messages

The following delegate summary is wrong. Listen to the voice messages and match the information to the delegates.

DELEGATES				
Name	**Occupation**	**Company**	**City**	**Contact no.**
Sonya GONIN	accountant	AC Computers	Brussels	070 36 4188 95
Ole BOYSEN	sales rep	PLP International	Sydney	073 6125 144

5 Application

Contact details

Make sure you can ask for contact details and say who you are. Talk to members of your group and then fill in this address book.

e.g. – Where are you from?
– I'm from London. I work for DTT.
– What do you do?
– I'm an IT consultant.

Family name:	....	....
First name:	....	....
Nationality:	....	....
Occupation:	....	....
Company:	....	....
Department:	....	....
Telephone:	....	....
(home)	....	....
(office)	....	....
(mobile)	....	....
Email:	....	....

Language notes

The Present tense: *to be*

Affirmative:
I am (I'm) …
He/She/It is (He's/She's/It's) …
We/You/They are (We're/You're/They're) …
e.g. He's an engineer.
We're from PLP International.

Negative:
I am (I'm) not …
He/She/It is (He's/She's/It's) not …
(He/She/It isn't) …
We/You/They are (We're/You're/They're) not …
(We/You/They aren't) …
e.g. She isn't in the sales department.
They aren't from KP Marketing.

Interrogative:
Am I …?
Is he/she/it …?
Are we/you/they …?
e.g. Is she a [sales rep]?
Are you [Tom Young]?

Short answers:

Yes I am.	No I'm not.
Yes, he/she/it is.	No, he's/she's/it's not.
	No, he/she/it isn't.
Yes, we/you/they are.	No, we're/you're/they're not.
	No, we/you/they aren't.

e.g. Are you [Tom Young]?
Yes, I am. / No, I'm not.

Note: the affirmative short answer is not contracted.
Yes, I am (not **Yes, I'm**).

a/an

We normally use *an* before a vowel – *a e i o u*.
e.g. **an** American company
an interesting job
an Italian name

We normally use *a* before other letters.
e.g. **a** department
a telephone number
a company

But notice that we say *a European company* (not *an European Company*). Notice also that we use *a* or *an* when we talk about occupations.
e.g. I am **a** sales representative.
She is **a** designer.
He is **an** IT consultant.
Are you **an** accountant?

Subject pronouns

Singular	Plural
I	we
you	you
he	they
she	they
it	they

e.g. Are you [Bill Smith]?
Yes, I am.

Telephone numbers

0 = zero/oh	5 = five
1 = one	6 = six
2 = two	7 = seven
3 = three	8 = eight
4 = four	9 = nine

- 'oh' is more common than 'zero' in phone numbers.
- 027 3144
  = oh two seven three one four four
  or
  = oh two seven three one double four

Titles

Write	Say	Example
Mr	mister	Mr Smith
Mrs	misses	Mrs Smith
Ms	merz	Ms Smith
Miss	miss	Miss Smith

Greetings

Good morning.
Good afternoon.
Good evening.

See also Language Notes in:
- Unit 7, Greetings

UNIT 2
About your job

1 Key dialogues

Overview

Listen to the dialogues (a–d) and answer the questions.

a What does he do?
Is he in the IT department?

b Does she work for a law firm?
Is she the finance director?

c Is she in the sales and marketing division?
Is she an engineer?

d Does she work for a company called Games Inc?
Does she like her job?

2 Study points

Check the Language Notes as you do these exercises.

The Simple Present tense

1 Write the verbs in brackets in the correct form. Then practise talking about a colleague, with a partner.

A: What **a** .... (do) Faisal Suri do?

B: **b** .... (he work) for a company called Matsu Engineering.

A: How **c** .... (you spell) Matsu?

B: M-A-T-S-U.

A: **d** .... (he be) an engineer?

B: Yes, but **e** .... (he not work) in Production.

A: **f** .... (he work) in R&D?

B: No, **g** .... (he not).
h .... (he be) on the training side.

A: What's he like? **i** .... (you like) him?

B: Yes, **j** .... (I …), but
k .... (I not know) him very well.

Object pronouns

2 Practise object pronouns by talking about your company. **Partner A** asks questions from the table. **Partner B** replies. Refer to the Language Notes for help.

Questions		Answers
Do you know	your chairman/chairperson/ managing director? the new advertising manager? the deputy assistant sales director? Mr/Mrs/Miss/Ms [Jones]? the sales staff?	Yes, I know .... very well. No, I don't know .... very well. Yes, I like .... very much. No, I don't like .... very much.
Do you like	your job/work/office/car? this/these?	

Spell check

3a Listen to the recording and correct the spelling of the company names.

       Erawan
a ~~Arownen~~ Manufacturing
b Nacanoshimer Engineering
c Keroona Oil
d Zugorski Trading
e Dolly Associates
f Loflider Industries
g Bracoled Services
h Screen-Quick Advertising

3b Check that you can answer these questions.
• How do you spell your name?
• What's your company called?
• How do you spell that?

Use of *the*

4 Refer to the Language Notes, then fill in the gaps using *the*, or *a/an*.

a Ed Martin is .... export sales manager.

b Eva Brant works for .... international law firm; she's .... lawyer.

c Vince and Pepe work on .... manufacturing side.

d Peter Lim works for .... software company in Hong Kong; he's .... deputy finance director.

e Is Tammy Sukiski in .... Purchasing?

f Do you work in .... sales department?

g Mrs Felou is .... assistant sales manager.

h We work for Inatia Systems, in .... European sales team.

3 Guided practice
Saying what you do

In pairs, use the flowchart to practise saying what you do.

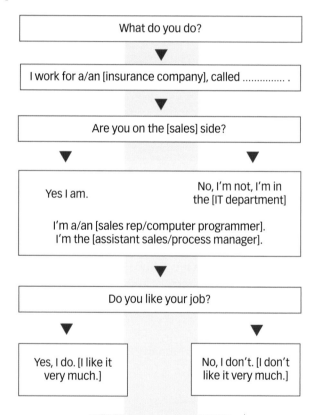

What do you do?

▼

I work for a/an [insurance company], called ....

▼

Are you on the [sales] side?

▼   ▼

Yes I am.   No, I'm not, I'm in the [IT department]

I'm a/an [sales rep/computer programmer]. I'm the [assistant sales/process manager].

▼

Do you like your job?

▼   ▼

Yes, I do. [I like it very much.]   No, I don't. [I don't like it very much.]

4 Application

Talking about work

Make sure you can talk about your work. Read the message below and then prepare a statement about yourself.

I work for a law firm called **TIFF Associates**. I'm not a lawyer. I'm on the finance side. It's a Japanese company, but I work in the Kuala Lumpur office. I'm Assistant Manager of the accounts department. I like my work very much.

Language notes

The Simple Present tense

Affirmative:
He/She/It works …
I/We/You/They work …
e.g. He works for a bank.
 I work in Sales.

Negative:
He/She/It does not (doesn't) work …
I/We/You/They do not (don't) work …
e.g. She doesn't work for Ufem.
 We don't work on the manufacturing side.

Interrogative:
Does he/she/it work …?
Do I/we/you/they work …?
e.g. Does he work for Saffer Security?
 Do you work in the legal department?

Short answers:
Yes, he/she/it does.   No, he/she/it doesn't.
Yes, I/we/you/they do.   No, I/we/you/they don't.
e.g. Do you work for Rhodes Associates?
 Yes, I do. / No, I don't.

Object pronouns

Singular: (I) me, (you) you, (he) him, (she) her, (it) it
Plural: (we) us, (you) you, (they) them
e.g. I like my job (it) very much.
 I like the new manager (him/her) very much.
 I do not (don't) work for Etaak (them).

Uses of *the*

Department names can be with or without **the**.
e.g. I work in **the** R&D department.
 or I work in R&D.
 (not *I work in R&D department.*)

Job titles can be with or without **the**.
e.g. I am **the** Finance Director.
 or I am Finance Director.

Generally, we use **the** to talk about particular things.
Compare: – I work in a team. (general)
 – I work in **the** service team. (particular)

 – I work for an IT company. (general)
 – I work for **the** company on the second floor. (particular)

UNIT 3 About where you work

1 Key dialogues

Overview

Listen to the dialogues (a–d) and answer the questions.

a Where is his office?
Is there a car park?

b Where does he work?
Do they have a canteen?

c Where is Moscow Road?
Is her department on the second floor?

d Where does he work?
Are there any good restaurants or cafes nearby?

2 Study points

Check the Language Notes as you do these exercises.

Numbers 1–100

1 Around the group, practise asking addresses and writing them down.

e.g. – What's your address?
– 67 Figeres Drive
– How do you spell that?
– F-I-G-E-R-E-S.
– And what's the area code?
– 17780.

Ordinal numbers up to tenth

2 Can you say these numbers?
Can you write them?

a 1st	**d** 5th ....
b 2nd	**e** 7th ....
c 3rd	**f** 9th ....

Practise using the numbers.

e.g. – Which floor are you on?
– Our offices are on the eighth floor.

Present tense of to have

3 Practise using the verb *to have* by asking about facilities.

Questions		Answers
Does your company have Does AC have Does it have Do you have	a cafeteria? a car park? a coffee machine a meeting room? a reception area? video conference facilities?	Yes, it does. (It's in the basement.) Yes, we do. (It's on the second floor.) No, it doesn't. No, we don't.

there is/are *and* some/any

4 Practise by making true statements about your area.

e.g. There is .... *a cafe near my office.* ....

There are .... *some nice shops not far from the station.* ....

a There are some ....

b There isn't a/an ....

c There aren't any ....

d .... a good restaurant near ....

e .... any bars in ....

f .... any ....

g .... a car park ....

3 Guided practice

Saying where you work

In pairs, use the flowchart to practise saying where you work.

Where do you work?

▼

I work in a/an [office/factory],
[in/near the centre of town].

▼

Are there any good [restaurants/cafes] nearby?

▼   ▼

Yes there are.   No, there aren't (But there
                                      is/are/a/some ....)

(And/But we have an excellent cafeteria/coffee shop.)

▼

We must meet for [lunch/a drink].

▼

Good/Nice/Excellent idea.

4 Listening

Arranging to meet

Listen to people talking about where they work and arranging to meet. Then study the information below and fill in the table.

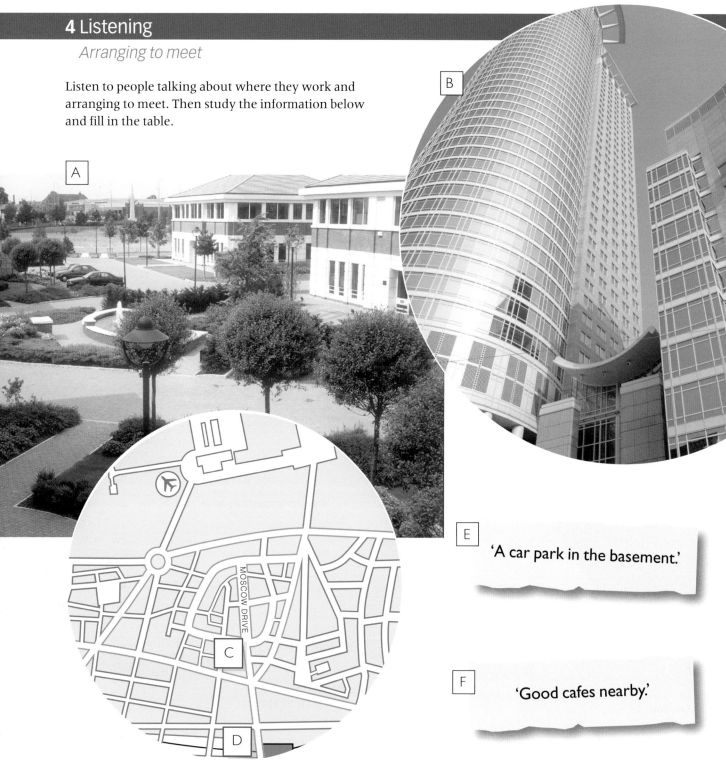

A

B

C

MOSCOW DRIVE

D

E

'A car park in the basement.'

F

'Good cafes nearby.'

Where do they work?			
	Building	**Location**	**Features**
Dialogue 1	....	....	....
Dialogue 2	....	....	....

5 Application

Giving details

Make sure you can give details of where you work. Read the message on the right and write one to a contact.

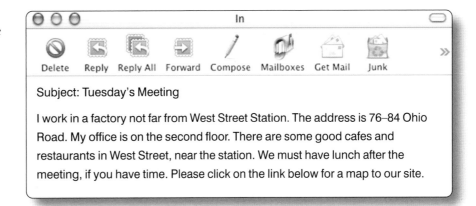

Subject: Tuesday's Meeting

I work in a factory not far from West Street Station. The address is 76–84 Ohio Road. My office is on the second floor. There are some good cafes and restaurants in West Street, near the station. We must have lunch after the meeting, if you have time. Please click on the link below for a map to our site.

Language notes

There is/are and some/any

Affirmative:
There is (There's) a/an …
There is (There's) some …
There are some …
e.g. There's some milk on the table.
    There are some shops nearby.

Negative:
There is not (isn't) any …
e.g. There isn't any coffee.
    There aren't any cafes near the airport.

Interrogative:
Is there a/an …?
Is there any …?
Are there any …?

Short answers:
Yes, there is.   No, there's not.
              No, there isn't.
Yes, there are. No, there aren't.
e.g. Are there any bars near your office?
    Yes, there are. / No, there aren't.

Notice that some nouns are 'countable' – we can count them:
one cafe; two cafes; some cafes.
Some nouns are 'uncountable' – we measure them:
some milk (not: a milk); a litre of milk; two litres of milk (not: some milks).

The Present tense: *to have*

Affirmative:
He/She/It has …
I/We/You/They have …
e.g. It has ten floors.
    We have a canteen.

Negative:
He/She/It does not (doesn't) have …
I/We/You/They do not (don't) have …
e.g. He doesn't have a secretary.
    They don't have a car park.

Interrogative:
Does he/she/it have …?
Do I/we/you/they have …?

Short answers:
Yes, he/she/it does.   No, he/she/it doesn't.
Yes, I/we/you/they do. No, I/we/you/they don't.
e.g. Does your warehouse have a car park?
    Yes, it does. / No, it doesn't.

Abbreviations

Road	Rd
Street	St
Avenue	Av
Drive	Dr

Cardinal numbers 1–100

1	one	20	twenty
2	two	21	twenty-one
3	three	22	twenty-two
4	four	23	twenty-three
5	five	24	twenty-four
6	six	25	twenty-five
7	seven	26	twenty-six
8	eight	27	twenty-seven
9	nine	28	twenty-eight
10	ten	29	twenty-nine
11	eleven	30	thirty
12	twelve	40	forty
13	thirteen	50	fifty
14	fourteen	60	sixty
15	fifteen	70	seventy
16	sixteen	80	eighty
17	seventeen	90	ninety
18	eighteen	100	a hundred
19	nineteen		

Ordinal numbers 1st–10th

1st	first	6th	sixth
2nd	second	7th	seventh
3rd	third	8th	eighth
4th	fourth	9th	ninth
5th	fifth	10th	tenth

UNIT 4
Your business activities

Focus

Expressions:
We make parts for computers. We are (We're) in the IT business.
We do a lot of business in Western Europe.
We're working on a new product.
Business is going well.

Prepare:
… to talk about your business activities.
When do you talk about your business activities?
What do you say to customers or colleagues?
If available, bring emails, brochures etc. to the class.
Refer to the unit Language Summary on page 123.

1 Key dialogues

Overview

Listen to the dialogues (a–d) and answer the questions.

a What do they make?
  Where do they do most of their business?

b What does the company do?
  How's business?

c Is he in the insurance business?
  Do they do much business in Australia?

d Are they in IT?
  What are they working on at the moment?

2 Study points

Check the Language Notes as you do these exercises.

Meeting an ex-colleague

1 Fill the gaps in the dialogue using:

  a *make, do*
  b *much, many, a lot of.*

  Then practise the dialogue with a partner.

  A: What are you doing here?

  B: I'm **a** .... some work for your
    computer department.

  A: Really? What are you **b** .... these
    days?

  B: I'm working for TSK Technology. We
    c .... computers.

  A: Oh, I see. Do you **d** ....
    e .... business with this company?

  B: No, not **f** ....

  A: Look, I'm **g** .... some coffee. Do you
    want some?

  B: Yes, please.
    (Drinking coffee.)

  A: And is business going well?

  B: We aren't **h** .... **i** .... money
    yet, but the company has **j** ....
    potential.

  A: Well, it's very good to see you.

Saying what people are doing

2 Answer the questions, using the prompts.

e.g. Hello. What are you doing here?

(wait/taxi)

I'm waiting for a taxi.

a How's business in the Far East?

(go/well)

....

b What is your team working on at the moment?

(develop/management information system)

....

c Is the company making a profit?

(make (not make)/a lot of money)

....

d Is Max here?

(work/Barcelona)

....

e What's Ana doing?

(write/email)

....

f Where's Mohammed?

(make/coffee)

....

g What are you doing at the moment?

....

h Do you know what your boss is doing?

....

Parts of the world: percentages

3 In pairs label the areas on the map. Then talk about markets, using the table.

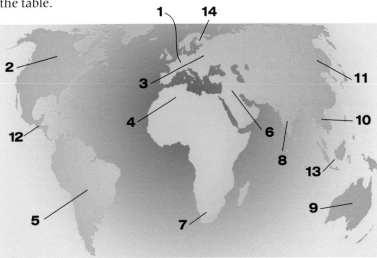

KEY	
North America	Southern Africa
Central America	The Middle East
South America	The Far East
South-East Asia	India
Asia Pacific	Eastern Europe
Australia	Western Europe
North Africa	Scandinavia

We do (about)	20% 60%	of our business in	North America.
XYZ does (about)	75% etc.	of its business in	South-East Asia.
We don't do	much	business in	The Middle East. etc.
They don't do	any		

3 Listening

Activities and markets

Listen to the recording and fill in the table.

Company	Main markets	Percentage of sales
Tektrom Computers Universal Trading Nexpol Insurance		

4 Guided practice

Business activities

In pairs, use the flowchart to practise talking about your business activities.

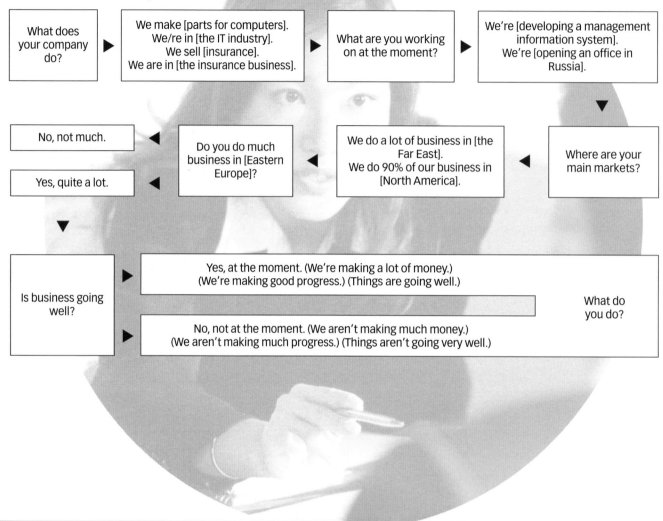

What does your company do?	▶	We make [parts for computers]. We/re in [the IT industry]. We sell [insurance]. We are in [the insurance business].

What are you working on at the moment? ▶ We're [developing a management information system]. We're [opening an office in Russia].

No, not much. ◀ Do you do much business in [Eastern Europe]? ◀ We do a lot of business in [the Far East]. We do 90% of our business in [North America]. ◀ Where are your main markets?

Yes, quite a lot. ◀

Is business going well? ▶ Yes, at the moment. (We're making a lot of money.) (We're making good progress.) (Things are going well.)

What do you do?

▶ No, not at the moment. (We aren't making much money.) (We aren't making much progress.) (Things aren't going very well.)

5 Application

Use what you know

Make sure you can talk about your business activities. Read this email and write one about your company.

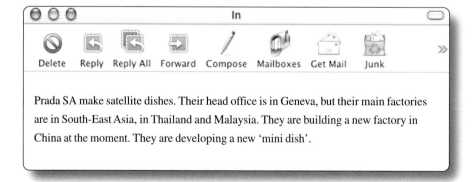

Prada SA make satellite dishes. Their head office is in Geneva, but their main factories are in South-East Asia, in Thailand and Malaysia. They are building a new factory in China at the moment. They are developing a new 'mini dish'.

The Present Continuous tense

Affirmative:

I am (I'm) working …
He/She/It is (He's/She's/It's) working …
We/You/They are (We're/You're/They're) working …

e.g. He's working in the Far East.
     We're working on a new range of products.

Negative:

I am not (I'm not) working …
He/She/It is not (He's/She's/It's not) working …
                 (He/She/It isn't) working …
We/You/They are not (We're/You're/They're not) working …
(We/You/They aren't working …)

e.g. It isn't working very well.
     They aren't working in this office.

Interrogative:

Am I working?
Is he/she/it working?
Are we/you/they working?

e.g. Is he working on the new information system?
     Are they working in the Middle East?

Short answers:

Yes, I am.	No, I'm not.
Yes, he/she/it is.	No, he's/she's/it's not.
	No, he/she/it isn't.
Yes, we/you/they are.	No, we're/you're/they're not.
	No, we/you/they aren't.

e.g. Are you working in the new factory?
     Yes, we are. / No, we aren't.

a lot of, much, many

Affirmative:

e.g. KCL export a lot of cars.
     There is a lot of money in our account.
     We employ a lot of people.
     We do a lot of business in the Middle East.

Negative:

e.g. They don't make many cars.
     There isn't much money in our account.
     We don't employ many people.
     We don't have much time.

Interrogative and short answers:

e.g. How many people are there in your department?
     (Quite) a lot.   Not very many.
     How much money have we got in our account?
     (Quite) a lot.   Not very much.
     Do you do much business in Western Europe?
     Yes, (quite) a lot.   No, not (very) much.
     Do KCL import many parts?
     Yes, (quite) a lot.   No, not (very) many.

make and do

Make means **create** or **construct**.

e.g. We make cars/parts for computers.
     They are making a lot of money
     Are they making a profit?
     I'm making coffee. Do you want some?

Use **do** to talk about activities, especially work.

e.g. What does your company do?
     We do a lot of business in Eastern Europe.
     We're doing some work in India at the moment.
     Miguel! What are you doing here?

UNIT 5 The location of your company

Focus

Expressions:
Our engineers' offices are five kilometres west of the city.
They are (They're) in Inchon.
It is (It's) about 300 kilometres from Pusan.
Where are your company's main offices?

Prepare:
… to talk about the location of your company.
When do you give directions to your company?
What do you need to say?
If available, bring maps and/or emails to the class.
Refer to the unit Language Summary on page 123.

1 Key dialogues

Overview

Listen to the dialogues (a–d) and answer the questions.

a Where are their offices in Japan?
b Where is the Malaysian agent's office?
c Where is the Vietnamese representative's office?
d Where are the Korean factories?

2 Study points

Check the Language Notes as you do these exercises.

Numbers 100–1000

1 Write out these numbers.

a 100	....	**e** 110	....
b 200	....	**f** 230	....
c 400	....	**g** 472	....
d 900	....	**h** 985	....

Compass points

2 Work with a partner to complete the map.

Partner A: You need to know where the places below are on the map.
Partner B: Your map has the information (see page 131).

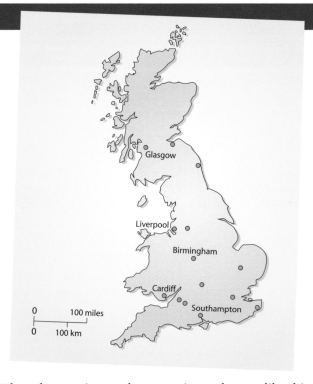

Edinburgh   Newcastle   Manchester   Bristol
Bath   Cambridge   Dover

e.g. Where's Bath?
   It's about 100 kilometres west of Oxford.

When the map is complete, practise exchanges like this.

e.g. – Our office is in Southampton.
   – Where's Southampton?
   – It's about 130 kilometres south-west of London.

Plural nouns

3 Change these sentences to make them plural.

e.g. We have a Spanish subsidiary.

(two) ....*We have two Spanish subsidiaries.*....

a It's a kilometre from here.

(350) ....

....

b It has a Spanish address.

....

....

....

c One man and one woman work there.

(120/250) ....

....

....

d One has a child.

(172) ....

....

....

e The man's wife works part time.

....

....

....

f She is an interesting person.

....

....

....

g This is a fax from our French factory?

....

....

....

h It is a photo of the staff.

....

....

....

Possessive nouns and adjectives

4 Practise in pairs using these tables.

Is	Your [John's] [Mary's] [Mary and John's]	office company warehouse home apartment	near here? in [Brussels]?

No,	my our his her their	office company warehouse home apartment	is [west] of the city, is to the [west] of the city, is five kilometres [west] of the city	in a place called … near a village called …

e.g. – Is your warehouse near here?
   – No, our warehouse is south of the city, near a place called …

   – Is Mary's company in Brussels?
   – No, her company is to the west of the city, in a town called …

3 Guided practice

Location

In pairs, use the flowchart to practise talking about where your company or your offices are.

Where is [your head office]?

Our head office is in [Inchon].

Where/Whereabouts is that?

It's about [40 kilometres west of Seoul]. (It's about .... kilometres to the north.)

Is it far from (Pusan)?

Yes, it is. (It's about .... kilometres from Pusan.)   No, it isn't far. (It's about .... kilometres away.)

And do you have [any distributors in Thailand]?

We have [one in the south-west of the country] [not far from ....].

4 Application

A presentation

Make sure you can talk about the location of your company. Listen to the presentation and put the bullet points in the right order. Then prepare a short presentation about your company.

THB Engineering

Overview

- Make parts for the car industry.
- Distributors in the north, south and east.
- Small engineering company.
- Workforce 220.
- Two factories in the west of the country.

Language notes

Possessive adjectives

Singular:

I	→	my
you	→	your
he	→	his
she	→	her
it	→	its

e.g. This is my colleague, John Snow.
His boss is in New York.

Plural:

we	→	our
you	→	your
they	→	their

e.g. Their managers are very good.
Our office is on the tenth floor.

Possessive nouns

Singular:

Mr Smith	→	Mr Smith's
the company	→	the company's
the chairman	→	the chairman's

e.g. Mr Smith's car
the chairman's office

Plural:

engineers	→	engineers'
customers	→	customers'
directors	→	directors'

e.g. the engineers' families
the directors' meeting

Numbers 100–1000

100	= one hundred or a hundred
300	= three hundred
306	= three hundred and six
556	= five hundred and fifty-six
999	= nine hundred and ninety-nine
1,000	= one thousand or a thousand

Compass points

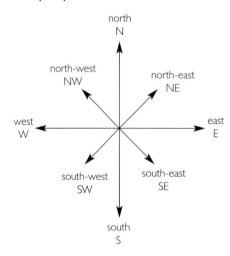

e.g. It is south (of the city).
It is to the south (of the city).
It is five kilometres south/to the south.
It is in the south (of the country).

Plurals of nouns

most nouns simply add -**s**:	manager	→	managers
	name	→	names
nouns ending in consonant + -**y**:	secretary	→	secretaries
	company	→	companies
nouns ending in -**ch**, -**sh**, -**s** or -**x**:	fax	→	faxes
	address	→	addresses
nouns ending in -**f** or -**fe**:	wife	→	wives
	life	→	lives
	half	→	halves
some nouns ending in -**f** and -**fe**:	safe	→	safes
	cliff	→	cliffs
irregulars:	child	→	children
	man	→	men
	woman	→	women
	potato	→	potatoes
	tomato	→	tomatoes
	tooth	→	teeth
	person	→	people

UNIT 6 The layout of your company

FOCUS

Expressions:
This is the service department.
Where is (Where's) the conference centre?
It is (It's) behind the main block.
Go down here. It's on the left.

Prepare:
… to talk about the layout of your company.
Do you show people round? When do you give visitors directions?
If possible, bring site plans and brochures to the class.
Refer to the unit Language Summary on page 124.

1 Key dialogues

Overview

Listen to the dialogues (a–d) and answer the questions.

a Are they in the main production building?
Where's the service department?

b Which floor is the accounts department on?
What's the visitor's name?

c Where are they?
Where's the help desk?

d Is the toilet upstairs or downstairs?
Is it the first or second door on the left?

2 Study points

Check the Language Notes as you do these exercises.

Understanding site plans

1 Make a simple site plan (of your company or another) and point out places on it. Work in pairs, asking and answering questions.

e.g. – What's this/that?
– That place is a warehouse.
– What are those buildings?
– Those are the main administration offices.
– Where's marketing and sales?
– In that building, on the third floor.

```
┌─────────────────────────────────────┐
│  ┌───┐        ┌───┐        ┌───┐     │
│  │ 1 │        │ 2 │        │ 3 │     │
│  └───┘        └───┘        └───┘     │
│  ┌───┐                               │
│  │ 4 │        ┌───┐                  │
│  └───┘        │ 5 │                  │
│  ┌───┐        └───┘        ┌───┐     │
│  │ 7 │                     │ 6 │     │
│  └───┘   ┌───┐             └───┘     │
│          │ 9 │                       │
│          └───┘                       │
└─────────────────────────────────────┘
```

Prepositions of place

2 Look at the diagram and complete these sentences.

a The cafeteria is .... the main block.

b It is .... the second floor.

c The main block is .... the main gate.

d .... behind ....

e .... between ....

f .... on the left of ....

g .... next to ....

h .... on the right of ....

1 Conference centre
2 Testing area
3 Paint shop
4 Car park
5 Main block (cafeteria, 2nd floor)
6 Main production building
7 Service and spares
8 Warehouse (Goods Inwards)
9 Main gate

Imperatives and prepositions of direction

3 Practise imperatives and prepositions of direction by giving directions:

    a to places inside a building – e.g. reception, your office, etc.

    b to places outside the building – e.g. the main gate, a cafe, etc.

Examples

Go Drive Walk	along up down	here/there. that path/road. the corridor.
Turn	left/right.	
It's They are	this/that way. upstairs/downstairs. on the left/right. over there. the first/second door/block	on the left/right.

---

3 Listening

Signing in

Visitors to ULT Ltd have to sign in at reception. Listen to two visitors and complete the signing-in book.

Name	Company	Visiting		Time in	Time out
		[Name]	[Department]		
Fanon	a	Mr Adam	b	10.30	
c	d	Mr Malick	e	10.37	

---

4 Practice

Site layout

Practise talking about layout.

Partner A: You are a visitor to GATT. Call **Partner B** to get the information missing from your plan.

Partner B: Turn to page 131 for your information.

    e.g. Where's the Service Centre?

        It's …

AB Main administration block
SC Service centre
TA Testing area
WS Warehouse and stores
     (Goods Inwards)
MG Main gate
CP Customer car park

PS Paint shop
SR Showroom/Reception
SP Staff car park
CC Conference centre and
     training department
PB Production building

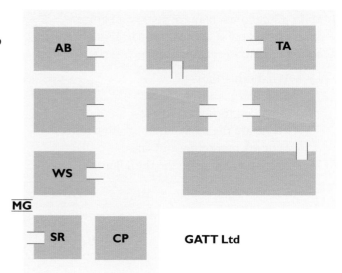

Showing people around

Make sure you can talk about the layout of your company. Using this flowchart, practise showing someone round. If possible, use the plan you brought to class or make a diagram.

This/That is the [main block/production building]. (These/Those are the administrative offices.)

What's [that place]? (What are these buildings?)

It's [the testing area]. (They're the warehouses.)

Where's [the accounts department]? (Where are your workshops)?

It's [opposite ....]. (They are behind ....)

How do I find it? How do I find them? Is it this way?

(Go along here. It's ....) (They're through ....) (Yes, it's ....)

Language notes

this/that/these/those

Here

Singular:

This is my secretary.
This is my office.
The paint shop is through this door.

Plural:

These people work in my department.
The toilet is up these stairs.

There

Singular:

That man is my CEO.
I work in that building.
That is our main production area.

Plural:

Marketing and Sales are in those buildings.
Those are the main administration offices.

Prepositions

Place

| in | on | next to | in front of |

| behind | opposite | between |

L R
on the left of   on the right of

Direction

| to | down | up |

| along | through | past |

Imperative

You form the imperative from the infinitive.

To go → Go along here.
To walk → Walk down the stairs.
To turn → Turn left/right.

You form the negative with **do not**.

e.g. Do not (Don't) go that way.
Do not (Don't) use the lift.
Do not (Don't) forget.

UNIT 7
Meeting and welcoming

Focus

Expressions:
I would (I'd) like to welcome you to KPG.
How was your trip?
It was fine.
This is Bill Smith, our PR Manager.
Pleased to meet you.

Prepare:
… to introduce yourself, and greet customers and colleagues.
Think of the situations when you do this.
If possible, bring your business diary to class.
Refer to the unit Language Summary on page 124.

1 Key dialogues

Overview

Listen to the dialogues (a–d) and answer the questions.

a Does Clare Hanan know the group?
How was their trip?

b Was her flight OK?
How was her hotel?

c How was his trip to Britain?
Were the hotel arrangements OK?

d Where is Mrs Walchia from?
Does she speak English?

2 Study points

Check the Language Notes as you do these exercises.

The Past tense of the verb to be

1 Think of a business or private trip. **Partner A** asks questions from the table. **Partner B** responds.

Questions			Answers
	the flight		Yes, it was.
	the journey		No, it wasn't.
	the hotel(s)		Yes, they were.
	the hotel arrangements		No, they weren't.
Was	the travel arrangements	OK?	
	the taxi(s)	good?	
Were	the plane	on time?	
	the weather	nice?	
	the timetable		
	the people		

was/wasn't and were/weren't

2 Make statements about the trip using *was/wasn't* or *were/weren't*.

a The hotel arrangements .... very good.

b The weather .... very nice.

c The plane(s) .... on time.

d The train .... clean.

e The travel arrangements .... very good.

f The people .... very friendly.

g The timetable .... very well organised.

h The hotel(s) .... very expensive.

a few *and* a little

3 Complete these examples using *a few* or *a little*.

a I understand .... Russian.

b I know .... words in Arabic.

c I saw .... old friends at the conference.

d There are .... cars in the car park.

e I have .... money.

f Would you like .... coffee?

g There are .... new people in my department.

Nationalities and languages

4 Using the Language Notes, complete the table.

Country	Nationality	Language
Brazil	**a**	Portuguese
b	British	English
China	Chinese	**c** ....
Egypt	Egyptian	**d** ....
e	French	French
Hungary	**f**	Hungarian
Japan	Japanese	**g** ....
h	Spanish	Spanish
United States	**i**	English

Now practise in pairs.

e.g. – Have you been to Brazil?
　　　– Yes, on business/on holiday?
　　　– Do you speak Portuguese?
　　　– I speak a little/I speak a few words.

3 Listening

People meeting

Listen to the people meeting. Do they know each other? Tick ✓ the right columns.

	Colleagues	Friends	First time
1st meeting			
2nd meeting			
3rd meeting			
4th meeting			

4 Guided practice

Introducing yourself

Using this flowchart, practise meeting someone and introduce yourself.

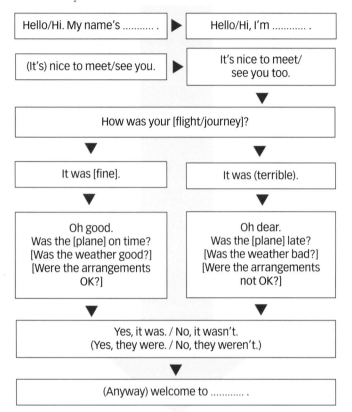

| Hello/Hi. My name's .... | ▶ | Hello/Hi, I'm .... |

| (It's) nice to meet/see you. | ▶ | It's nice to meet/ see you too. |

| How was your [flight/journey]? |

| It was [fine]. | | It was (terrible). |

| Oh good. Was the [plane] on time? [Was the weather good?] [Were the arrangements OK?] | | Oh dear. Was the [plane] late? [Was the weather bad?] [Were the arrangements not OK?] |

| Yes, it was. / No, it wasn't. (Yes, they were. / No, they weren't.) |

| (Anyway) welcome to .... |

5 Application

At a reception

Make sure you know the language you need when you meet new people, and when you greet people you know. Imagine you are at a reception with the rest of the group.

Some you know.	→	Greet them.
Some you don't know.	→	Introduce yourself.
Some are back from a trip.	→	Ask about it.

Language notes

The Past tense of *to be*: was/were

Affirmative:
I/He/She/It was ...
We/You/They were ...
e.g. It was a good trip.
　　 They were in London.

Negative:
I/He/She/It was not (wasn't) ...
We/You/They were not (weren't) ...
e.g. She wasn't on time.
　　 They weren't OK.

Interrogative:
Was I/he/she/it ...?
Were we/you/they ...?
e.g. Was he French?
　　 Were they from Italy?

Short answers:
Yes, I/he/she/it was.
No, I/he/she/it wasn't.
Yes, we/you/they were.
No, we/you/they weren't.
e.g. Was the hotel good?
　　 Yes, it was. / No, it wasn't.

few/little

I speak **a little** English.
I know **a few** words.

Use *a little* with things you can't count.
e.g. **a little** time
　　 a little money
　　 a little coffee

Use *a few* with things you can count.
e.g. **a few** hours
　　 a few dollars
　　 a few colleagues

Greetings

Hello/Hi
Good morning (before lunch)
Good afternoon (after lunch)
Good evening (after about 18.00)

Some nationalities and languages

Can you say your nationality in English?

Country	Nationality	Language
Brazil	Brazilian	Portuguese
Britain	British	English
China	Chinese	Chinese
Egypt	Egyptian	Arabic
France	French	French
Romania	Romania	Romania
Japan	Japanese	Japanese
Russia	Russian	Russian
Spain	Spanish	Spanish
United States	American	English

UNIT 8 The first two minutes

Focus

Expressions:
How are you? How is (How's) business?
How do you like New York?
How long are you here for?
I hear you are (you're) leaving tomorrow.

Prepare:
… to practise the first two minutes when meeting a contact.
What do you talk about when you first meet people?
What do you talk about when you meet a colleague you don't know well?
Refer to the unit Language Summary on page 124.

1 Key dialogues

Overview

Listen to the dialogues (a–d) and answer the questions.

a How's Freya?
How are her family?

b When is he leaving?
Is he doing anything tomorrow evening?

c How does he like New York?
How long is he in New York for?

d How is business?
Is she leaving?

2 Study points

Check the Language Notes as you do these exercises.

The Present Continuous tense

1 Write sentences using the prompts to help you.

a What are you doing this afternoon?
(play/tennis) ....

b How are you getting home?
(drive) ....

c (When/you/see/Brenda)
....?

At two o'clock.

d (Where/we/have/lunch)
....?

At a French restaurant.

e (Is/Fiona/come/to the meeting)
....?

No, she isn't.

f (When/you/leave)
....?

After the lesson.

g When are you going on holiday?
....?

The use of hear/believe/see/understand + *future*

2 Using the Language Notes for help, practise talking about plans you already know about.
Complete the sentences, then practise in pairs.

a (you/meet/Diego/this afternoon)   I understand ....

b (you/go/Vienna/tomorrow)   I hear ....

c (Tom/arrive/Wednesday afternoon)   I see ....

d (we/meet/distributor/this evening)   I hear ....

e (you/fly/home/tomorrow morning)   I believe ....

f (you/drive/Rome/this afternoon)   I hear ....

g (Lara/meet/us/lunch)   I believe ....

Days of the week and parts of the day

3 Work in pairs to find out your
partner's plans for:

a tomorrow morning
b tomorrow afternoon
c Tuesday evening
d Friday afternoon
e Saturday/Sunday

e.g. What are you doing
tomorrow morning?

3 Guided practice

Starting a conversation

Using the flowchart to help you, practise starting a conversation. Work in pairs.

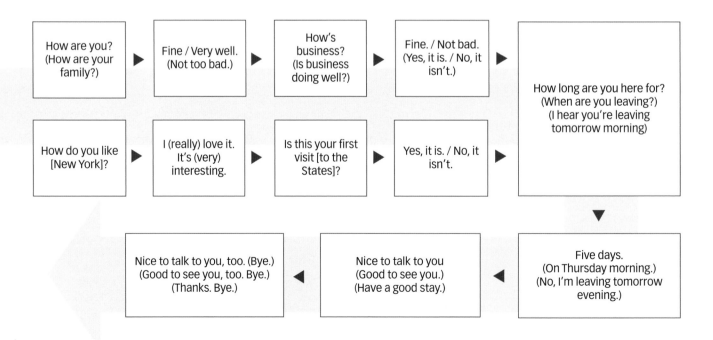

4 Listening

Visitors to Sydney

Listen to two Australians talking to business visitors to Sydney. Tick ✓ the right visitor.

	Visitor 1	Visitor 2
The speaker knows the visitor.		
The visitor is leaving on Thursday.		
The visitor's company has a sales office in Sydney.		
The visitor is meeting a distributor.		
The visitor is an IT consultant.		
The visitor's family is well.		
The visitor will send an email next time he/she is coming.		
The visitor really likes Sydney.		

5 Application

Talking to contacts

Make a dialogue from the examples in the two boxes. Then think about the people you meet and the real situations at work, and change the dialogue. Now practise in pairs.

Partner A	Partner B
– Well, it's nice to talk to you. – How long are you here for? – Are you from the Madrid office? – When are you leaving? – How do you like Tokyo?	– Four days. I'm doing a course at the academy. – It's nice to talk to you too. – On Tuesday evening. – Yes, I am. – Thanks. – I really like it.

Language notes

Days of the week

Monday (Mon)
Tuesday (Tues)
Wednesday (Wed)
Thursday (Thurs)
Friday (Fri)
Saturday (Sat)
Sunday (Sun)

Parts of the day

morning   evening
afternoon   night
e.g. in the morning
     this afternoon
     in the evening
     tomorrow morning
     on Monday morning
     tomorrow evening
     on Tuesday evening
     tonight

I hear/I believe

We use *I hear*, *I understand*, *I see*, etc. when we already know about a plan.
e.g. I understand you're leaving tomorrow morning.
     I believe they are coming at five.
     I see (in the newsletter) you are moving to Rome.
     I hear Sara is leaving the company.

UNIT 9
Partings and thanks

1 Key dialogues

Overview

Listen to the dialogues (a–d) and fill in the gaps.

a – Thanks for the lunch.
  – ....
  – And I'll see you next week.
  – ....
  – Bye.

b – Have a good flight.
  – ....
  – Well, thank you for coming.
  – Don't forget to keep in touch.
  – ....
  – Bye.

c – Give my regards to your MD.
  – ....
  – OK. Bye then. See you soon.
  – ....

d – Thanks for your help.
  – ....
  – I will.
  – ....
  – I'll email them tomorrow.
  – Keep in touch.

2 Study points

Check the Language Notes as you do these exercises.

will *in promises*

1 Fill in the gaps in these examples. Then in pairs practise exchanges like this.

e.g. – I'll see you at Christmas. Thanks for everything.
   – You are very welcome. See you at Christmas.

a I'll see you .... Christmas.

b I'll contact you .... the summer.

c I'll call you .... April.

d I'll send you an invitation .... the autumn.

e I'll visit you .... the New Year.

f I'll write to you .... February.

g I'll email a reminder .... Carnival time.

h I'll visit you .... Ramadan.

Invitations and requests

2 Write examples of invitations using 'must' in Box 1. Write examples of requests using the imperative in Box 2.

Now, in pairs, practise using the examples.

e.g. – You must visit us again.
– Thank you. I'd like to.
– Call me next week.
– I will.

Box 1

You must visit us again.
We must meet for dinner.
You must bring your family.

....

....

....

Box 2

Call me next week.
Give my regards to your wife.
Don't forget to send the report.

....

....

....

---

3 Guided practice

Saying goodbye

Using the phrases in the flowchart, practise saying goodbye.

Thanks for everything.
(Thank you for your help.)
(Many thanks for the lunch.)

It's my pleasure.
(No problem.)
(You're very welcome.)

I'll call you [next week].
(I'll see you in the New Year.)

Call me [on Monday].
(Don't forget to call.)
(Keep in touch.)

Right. / OK.

I will. / I won't.

Have a good flight. / Have a good journey.
(Give my regards to .... / Remember me to ....)

Thank you. I will.

You must visit us again (soon).
(See you soon.)
(Goodbye. / Bye.)

And you must come and visit us.
(See you.)
(Bye.)

---

4 Listening

Partings

Listen to the dialogues (a–d) and fill in the table below.

✓ = true
✗ = false
? = unclear

Dialogues	a	b	c	d
They are meeting next week.	✓	✗	✗	✗
They will talk next week.				
The visitor is flying home.				
The visitor is driving home.				
The visitor works on the sales side.				
The visitor works in production.				
They meet regularly.				
They work for the same company.				
They work in the same building.				
They will keep in touch.				

5 Application

Writing messages

Make sure you can say thank you and goodbye.

a Think of a situation at work. Then practise in pairs.

b Read the message. Then write an email you might send to a colleague or client.

Subject: Thanks

Hello Emma

Many thanks for all your help when I was in Rio. It was very good to see you. I attach the new figures, as promised. You must come to Poland next time you are in Europe. I'll see you at the Sales Conference. Give my regards to your team.

Best wishes,

Yuri

Language notes

Imperatives

Affirmative:

Call me …

Give …

e.g. Call me this evening.
       Give my regards to your MD.

Negative:

Do not (Don't) call me …

Do not (Don't) forget …

e.g. Don't call me tomorrow.
       Don't forget to call.

must for inviting

Singular:

I/You/He/She/It must …

Plural:

We/You/They must …

e.g. You must visit us again.
       We must meet for lunch.
       You must try this.

will in promises

– Call me on Monday.

– I will. (= a promise)

– Don't forget to send the report.

– I won't. (= a promise)

I will email the figures on Monday.
(= a promise)

I will see you in the spring.
(= a promise)

Months of the year

January (Jan)	July (Jul)
February (Feb)	August (Aug)
March (Mar)	September (Sept)
April (Apr)	October (Oct)
May (May)	November (Nov)
June (Jun)	December (Dec)

e.g. I will (I'll) see you in January.
       I will (I'll) see you this January.
       I will (I'll) see you next January.

Seasons of the year

in (the) spring
         summer
         autumn (fall in US English)
         winter

Festivals

(at) Easter

(in) the New Year

(at) Christmas

(on) Independence Day

(during) Ramadan

(at) Carnival Time

(at) Chinese New Year

e.g. I will (I'll) see you …
       … in the spring.
       … at Easter.
       … in the New Year.

UNIT 10
Setting up a meeting

Focus

Expressions:
Are you free tomorrow?
Can you make Friday?
I will (I'll) see you at four o'clock.
I am (I'm) afraid I cannot (can't) make it.

Prepare to:
… set up a meeting.
What meetings do you attend? Where and when are they?
Who attends?
If possible, bring details of your meetings – agendas, email messages etc.
Refer to the unit Language Summary on page 124.

1 Key dialogues
Overview

Listen to the dialogues (a–d) and answer the questions.

a Will he be free on the 13th?
And the 12th?

b Can he make Tuesday?
What about Wednesday?

c Can they meet in the morning?
What time will they meet?

d Is the 20th OK?
What day is the 20th

2 Study points

Check the Language Notes as you do these exercises.

Ordinal numbers, and dates and years

1 Can you say the following? Can you write them?

a 21st ....

b 70th ....

c 82nd ....

d 100th ....

e 3/7/97 ....

f 4th Oct ....

g 1/2/09 ....

h 28th March ....

Telling the time

2 Fill in the gaps.

a 1.15 ....*one fifteen*........

b .... six twenty-five

c .... ten fifty

d 9.30 ....

e 11.45 ....

f .... two twenty

g .... twelve forty

h 10.00 ....

Prepositions of time

3 Practise prepositions by filling in the gaps.

 a I'll see you .... three o'clock.

 b I'll see you .... Wednesday.

 c I can make it .... the morning.

 d I can't make it .... Tuesday afternoon.

 e I can't make it .... 19th November.

 f We can meet .... December.

 g I can't make it .... 3.30.

 h Can you make it .... the afternoon?

 i No, but I'm free .... the morning.

can

4 In pairs, practise arranging a time using this table.

Can	you	make	a meeting	on ...?
	your boss	come to	a conference	at ...?
	your			
	colleagues	attend	a party	in ...?

e.g. – Can you make a meeting at 3.15 on Wednesday?
  – No, I'm afraid I can't.
  – What/How about 4.15 on Thursday?

3 Guided practice

Arrangements to meet

Using the flowchart, make arrangements to meet. Work in pairs.

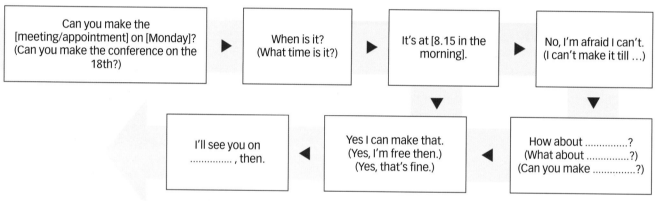

4 Listening

Confirming arrangements

When Dan Lustig receives the first email you can see from his boss, Lucy Kavanah, he calls her. Listen to the phone conversation and then correct the draft message prepared by Lucy Kavanah's assistant after the call.

(Draft)

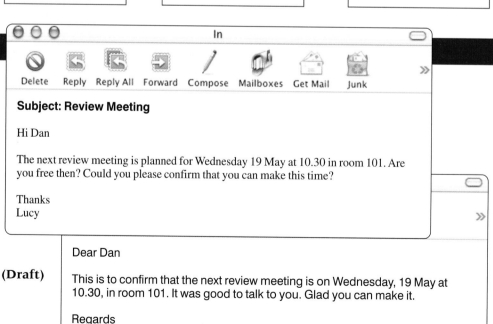

Subject: Review Meeting

Hi Dan

The next review meeting is planned for Wednesday 19 May at 10.30 in room 101. Are you free then? Could you please confirm that you can make this time?

Thanks
Lucy

Dear Dan

This is to confirm that the next review meeting is on Wednesday, 19 May at 10.30, in room 101. It was good to talk to you. Glad you can make it.

Regards
Lucy

5 Application

Using the language you need

Make sure you can set up meetings. Practise by replying to this message.

1 Write a reply …

   a … saying 'yes'.
   e.g. Dear …

   b … saying 'no' and suggesting a different time (or day).
   e.g. Dear …
       I'm afraid …

2 Look at your diary and note the times when you are free. Then arrange a time:

   a To meet a study partner
   b For the group to meet.
   e.g. – Can we meet today at 5.30?
       – I'm afraid I can't make that.
       – What about …?

Dear …………
I'm afraid I can't make the meeting on Wednesday morning. I'm not free till 2 pm. What about 11 o'clock on Thursday?

Best regards
……………

Language notes

can

Affirmative:
I/We/You/They can make …
He/She/It can come …
e.g. They can come to the meeting.
   John can't make it.

Negative:
I/We/You/They cannot (can't) make …
He/She/It cannot (can't) come …
e.g. I can't make the conference.
   She can't come to the presentation.

Interrogative:
Can I/we/you/they make …?
Can he/she/it come …?
e.g. Can you make 9.30?
   Can he come on Monday?

Short answers:
Yes, I/we/you/they can.
No, I/we/you/they can't.
Yes, he/she/it can.
No, he/she/it can't.
e.g. Can you make it on Friday?
   Yes, I can. / No, I can't.

Note: *can't* = cannot (written as one word)

make with arrangements

e.g. I can make five o'clock,
   He can make the afternoon.
   We can't make the 27th
   Can you make Monday?

When *make* has an object (*the meeting, it,* etc.), we must use a proposition.
e.g. I can make the meeting **at** five o'clock.
   He can make it **in** the afternoon.
   We can't make the conference **on** the 27th.
   Can you make the meeting **in** June?

Ordinal numbers 11th–100th

11th	eleventh	24th	twenty-fourth
12th	twelfth	25th	twenty-fifth
13th	thirteenth	26th	twenty-sixth
14th	fourteenth	27th	twenty-seventh
15th	fifteenth	28th	twenty-eighth
16th	sixteenth	29th	twenty-ninth
17th	seventeenth	30th	thirtieth
18th	eighteenth	40th	fortieth
19th	nineteenth	50th	fiftieth
20th	twentieth	60th	sixtieth
21st	twenty-first	70th	seventieth
22nd	twenty-second	80th	eightieth
		90th	ninetieth
23rd	twenty-third	100th	hundredth

Times and dates

At 12 o'clock (twelve o'clock)
At 2.15 (two fifteen) in the morning
At 5.30 (five thirty) in the afternoon
At 8.50 (eight fifty) in the evening
At 10.45 (ten forty-five) at night
On the 16th of September
On September the 16th

25th April / 25 April = the twenty-fifth of April.
April 25th / April 25 = April the twenty-fifth.

1/2/06 = the first of February, two thousand and six
(American English: the second of January, two thousand and six.)

9/8/03 = the ninth of August, two thousand and three.
(American English: the eighth of September, two thousand and three.)

1442 = fourteen forty-two
1998 = nineteen ninety-eight
2001 = two thousand and one
2009 = two thousand and nine
2021 = two thousand and twenty-one

UNIT 11
Confirming arrangements

Focus

Expressions:
I am (I'm) calling to confirm Tuesday's meeting.
Are you still OK for Monday?
Can I check the time?
Do you know where it is (yet)?

Prepare:
… to confirm the arrangement you make.
Who do you make arrangements with?
Do you have to confirm arrangements in English?
If possible, bring your diary and emails relating to arrangements to class.
Refer to the unit Language Summary on page 125.

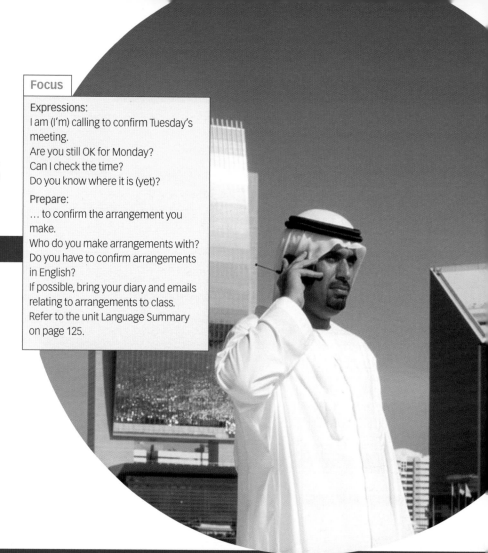

1 Key dialogues

Overview

Listen to the dialogues (a–d) and answer the questions.

a When is the meeting?
Is it in Petra's office?

b Is he still OK for Monday?
What time is the meeting?

c Is the meeting in the morning?
Where is it?

d Why is he calling?
Can she still make the meeting?

2 Study points

Check the Language Notes as you do these exercises.

Embedded/indirect questions

1 Practise embedded questions by checking the day, time and place of the arrangements listed in the table below.

Partner A: Talk to **Partner B**, who has the details.
Partner B: Your information is on page 131.

Do you know Can you check	what time (when) what day (when) where	the meeting is? the appointment is? our lunch is?
	if	it is at 7pm?

eg **Partner A:** Do you know what time the meeting is?
   Partner B: Yes, it's at ….

still or yet

2 Rewrite these sentences using *still* or *yet*.

e.g. I work for DTT.
(still) .... I still work for DTT. ....

a Do you know if you can come?
(yet) ....

b Are you coming to the meeting?
(still) ....

c Do you know where the meeting is?
(yet) ....

d I don't know when the meeting is.
(still) ....

e Is he back from lunch?
(yet) ....

f I don't know his name.
(still) ....

to *and* in order to

3 Practise *to* and *in order to* by making examples from the table.

e.g. I'm phoning to thank you for all your hospitality.

Then, in pairs, practise exchanges like this.
– Why are you phoning?
– To thank you for all your hospitality.

Actions	Aims
phoning	thank you for all your hospitality
writing	confirm the meeting
flying to [Japan]	visit customer
go to airport	meet a customer
building a factory	increase production
developing new products	improve profits

What are you doing at the moment? What is the aim?
e.g. I'm studying English to improve my career.

3 Listening

Confirming a schedule

Listen to the recording and fill in the gaps in the draft schedule.

Charlie Amosu, executive vice president (Europe), is visiting a subsidiary. His secretary calls to confirm the arrangements.

DRAFT SCHEDULE

Visit of Charlie Amosu, Executive Vice President

9.30 a.m   Meeting with Victoria Seren, **a** ....
Finance Director

b ....   Coffee with Management   Boardroom
Committee

c ....   Meeting with Peter Sallis,   **d** ....
Sales Director

4 Guided practice

Arrangements and meetings

In pairs, use the flowchart to practise making and confirming arrangements.

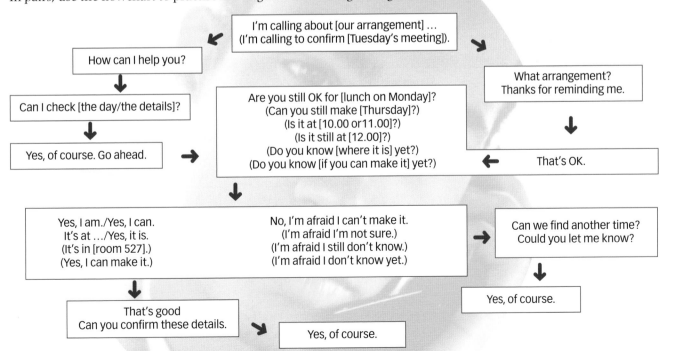

I'm calling about [our arrangement] …
(I'm calling to confirm [Tuesday's meeting]).

How can I help you?

What arrangement?
Thanks for reminding me.

Can I check [the day/the details]?

Yes, of course. Go ahead.

Are you still OK for [lunch on Monday]?
(Can you still make [Thursday]?)
(Is it at [10.00 or 11.00]?)
(Is it still at [12.00]?)
(Do you know [where it is] yet?)
(Do you know [if you can make it] yet?)

That's OK.

Yes, I am./Yes, I can.
It's at …/Yes, it is.
(It's in [room 527].)
(Yes, I can make it.)

No, I'm afraid I can't make it.
(I'm afraid I'm not sure.)
(I'm afraid I still don't know.)
(I'm afraid I don't know yet.)

Can we find another time?
Could you let me know?

Yes, of course.

That's good
Can you confirm these details.

Yes, of course.

5 Application

Using what you know

In pairs, confirm the following meetings.

Partner A: You are the organiser. Your information is in the table.

Partner B: You are attending. Your information is on page 131.

Confirm some of the details by phone and some by email.

Meetings	Time	Room
Tuesday's meeting	8.00 am.	B25
Wednesday's meeting	10.00	318
Friday's meeting	........*7.30 pm.*........	146
Saturday's meeting	9.30 am.	208

Confirming by phone

Partner B: What time is Tuesday's meeting? Is it still at 11.00?

Partner A: Yes, it is.

Partner B: Do you know the room yet?

Partner A: ....

Confirming by email

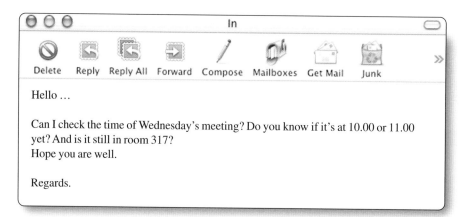

Hello …

Can I check the time of Wednesday's meeting? Do you know if it's at 10.00 or 11.00 yet? And is it still in room 317?
Hope you are well.

Regards.

Language notes

still and *yet*

Yet normally comes at the end of a sentence.

e.g. Do you know where it is **yet**?
Do you know if you can make it **yet**?
Are they ready **yet**?

Still normally comes before the (main) verb.

e.g. Can you **still** make it?
She **still** works for ETP.
Do you **still** want a coffee?

But *still* comes after the verb *to be*.

e.g. Are you **still** OK for Monday?
Is the meeting **still** at 10?
Mr Coots is **still** in Rome.

Direct and embedded questions

Direct	When is it?
Embedded	Do you know **when it is**?
Direct	Where is it?
Embedded	Can I check **where it is**?
Direct	Who is she?
Embedded	Can you tell me **who she is**?
Direct	Can you make the meeting?
Embedded	Can you tell me **if you can make the meeting**?

to/in order to

I'm calling **to** confirm our meeting.
= I'm calling **in order to** confirm our meeting.

He's going **to** Turkey to see the new factory.
= He's going to Turkey **in order** to see the new factory.

Time: am/pm

am = Before 12 o'clock in the middle of the day

pm = After 12 o'clock in the middle of the day

e.g. at 4.30 am
at 8 am
at 6 pm
at 7.15 pm

UNIT 12 Changing plans

1 Key dialogues

Key dialogues

Listen to the dialogues (a–d) and answer the questions.

a Is the conference room booked?
When will it be free?

b What's the problem?
Will the boardroom be free by ten?

c Is the room reserved?
Where are they meeting?

d Why can't John make the meeting?
What's the new time for the meeting?

2 Study points

Check the Language Notes as you do these exercises.

will/will not

1 Make true statements using the table below.

I My boss My secretary My colleagues	will be won't be in the office	away in [Zurich] next [Tuesday]. back from [Paris] free	tomorrow. this [Monday]. at [ten]. by [eleven].

In pairs, practise short answers.
e.g. – Will you be in your office tomorrow?
– Yes, I will. / No, I won't.
– Will your boss be away on Friday?
– Yes, he/she will. / I don't know.

have to

2 Which of these things do you have to do? Complete the examples, using the Language Notes for help.

e.g. *I have to* understand Greek.
I don't have to speak it.

a .... speak English in my job.

b .... read French at work.

c .... write emails in German.

d .... use English on the phone.

e .... speak Arabic with customers.

f .... write reports in English.

g .... understand instructions in Japanese.

h .... visit India.

Suggestions

3 Listen to the recording and match the speakers with the suggestions.

'The conference room is booked.'

a   An Egyptian importer.
b   A Swiss managing director.
c   A Welsh IT manager.
d   A Sierra Leonean administrative assistant.
e   A Canadian HR manager.

   i   'How about meeting in room number 12?'
  ii   'Could we try Room 8 instead?'
 iii   'Is there another room we can use?'
  iv   'Why don't we meet after lunch?'
   v   'Let's try to book another room.'

In pairs, think of a planned event. Then suggest changes – because the room is booked or someone can't make it.

why *and* because

4 Work in pairs. Arrange a time to meet.

Partner A: Your information is below.
Partner B: Your information is on page 131.

e.g. – Let's meet on Monday.
  – I'm afraid I can't.
  – Why (not)? (What's the problem?)
  – Because …
  – Why don't we …?

MON	on holiday
TUES	
WED	room booked
THUR	
FRI	in Zurich
SAT	

3 Guided practice

Changes

Using the flowchart, practise changing arrangements. Work in pairs.

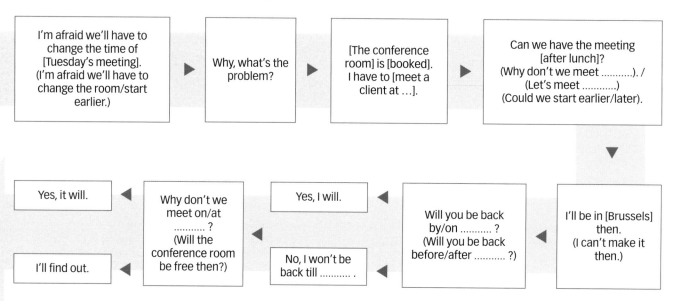

I'm afraid we'll have to change the time of [Tuesday's meeting]. (I'm afraid we'll have to change the room/start earlier.) ▶ Why, what's the problem? ▶ [The conference room] is [booked]. I have to [meet a client at …]. ▶ Can we have the meeting [after lunch]? (Why don't we meet ………..). / (Let's meet …………) (Could we start earlier/later).

▼

Yes, it will. ◀ Why don't we meet on/at ………… ? (Will the conference room be free then?) ◀ Yes, I will. ◀ Will you be back by/on ……….. ? (Will you be back before/after ……….. ?) ◀ I'll be in [Brussels] then. (I can't make it then.)

I'll find out. ◀ | No, I won't be back till ………… . ◀

4 Application

Relate the language back to your needs

Listen to the phone conversation and correct this email.

Think of the arrangements you make and write a similar email.

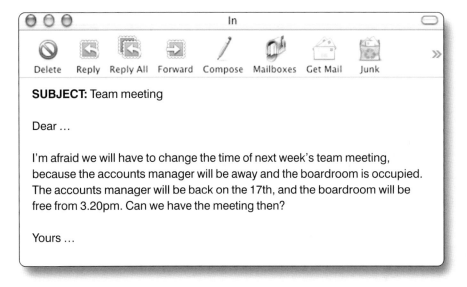

SUBJECT: Team meeting

Dear …

I'm afraid we will have to change the time of next week's team meeting, because the accounts manager will be away and the boardroom is occupied. The accounts manager will be back on the 17th, and the boardroom will be free from 3.20pm. Can we have the meeting then?

Yours …

Language notes

will/won't

Affirmative:

I/He/She/It will (I'll/He'll/She'll) be …
We/You/They will (We'll/You'll/They'll) be …

e.g. I'll be back by ten.
They'll come on Monday.

Negative:

I/He/She/It will not (won't) be …
We/You/They will not (won't) be …

e.g. He won't be back before lunch.
They won't come till Friday.

Interrogative:

Will I/he/she/it be …?
Will we/you/they be …?

e.g. Will you be free by ten?
Will they come back?

Short answers:

Yes, I/he/she/it will.   No, I/he/she/it won't.
Yes, we/you/they will. No, we/you/they won't.

e.g. Will you be here on Thursday?
Yes, I will. / No, I won't.

has to/have to

We will have to change the room.
We will have to start earlier.

have to/has to = obligation

e.g. I **have to** start work at 8 o'clock.
I do not (don't) **have to** speak Russian in my job.
She **has to** call clients in Sierra Leone.
He does not (doesn't) **have to** wear a suit.

Making suggestions

Let's	meet on Tuesday instead (?)
Why don't we We could Could we	book another room (?) try room 8 (?) start earlier/later (?)
How about	meeting on Tuesday instead?
What about	booking another room? trying room 8? Starting earlier/later?

why and because

Why can't we start at 9 o'clock?
Because the room is occupied at 9 o'clock.
We can't start at 9 o'clock because the room is occupied.

Why don't we meet on Wednesday?
Because I'm away on Wednesday.
We can't meet on Wednesday because John is away.

UNIT 13 Dealing with the unexpected

1 Key dialogues

Overview

Listen to the dialogues (a–d) and answer the questions.

a What's the problem?
When can they deliver?

b What's the problem?
What does the caller want?

c What's the problem?
What is the caller going to do?

d What's the first problem?
What's the second problem?

2 Study points

Check the Language Notes as you do these exercises.

going to

1 Complete the sentences below to make true statements using *going to*.

e.g. ....*I'm going to*.... visit Moscow ..*one day.*..
....*I'm not going to*.... visit Moscow ..*this year.*..

a .... drive through Spain ....

b .... fly to India ....

c .... meet the CEO ....

d .... work in the States ....

e .... change my job ....

f .... make a lot of money ....

In pairs, practise short answers using this table.

Questions				Answers	
Are	you	going to work (overtime)	this evening?	Yes, I am.	No, I'm not.
Is	your boss	going to be busy	on Monday/Tuesday?	Yes, he is.	No, he isn't.
	your secretary	going to study English	on Wednesday evening?	Yes, they are.	(I don't know.)
	your colleagues	etc.			

Phrasal verbs: call off/put off

2 In pairs, practise using *call off* and *put off*.

Partner A asks about arrangements.
Partner B tries to cancel or postpone them.

e.g. – Are you OK for Monday's meeting?
    – No. Can we put it off till next week?
or – Can we call it off? I'm going to be very busy on Monday.

too *and* either

3 In pairs, practise using *too* and *either*. Use the Language Notes for help.

I'm ill. I'm ill too.	I have a cold. I have one too.	I work in an office. I work in an office too.

I'm not well. I'm not well either.	I don't like meetings. I don't like them either.

Use verbs like: *am (am not), have (have not), like (don't like), work (don't work), make (don't make), speak (can't speak).*

could

4 Practise making requests using *could*. Work in pairs.

Could	you we I your team your colleagues your manager	.... ? .... ? .... ? .... ? .... ? .... ?

I'm calling to ask/see if	you we I your team your colleagues your manager	could	.... ? .... ? .... ? .... ? .... ? .... ?

e.g. – Could we postpone the meeting?
    – What's the problem?

    – I'm calling to see if we could postpone the meeting?
    – What's the problem?

3 Listening

Unexpected problems

Listen to the dialogues (a–c) and match the arrangement:

i with the reason for cancelling or postponing (d–f)
ii with the new arrangement (g–i).

Arrangement	Unexpected problem	New arrangement
a Tomorrow's deadlines **b** Conference call with Detroit **c** Lunch date	**d** Motorway blocked **e** IT problems **f** Security alert	**g** This afternoon **h** Next week **i** Another two days

4 Guided practice

Traffic jams, security alerts, etc.

Using this flowchart, practise dealing with unexpected problems. Work in pairs.

```
┌─────────────────────────────────────────────────┐
│   I'm calling about [the meeting].              │
│   (Can/Could we put it off/call it off?)        │
│   (I'm calling to ask if we could postpone      │
│    it/cancel it.)                               │
│   (I'm afraid I'm/we're not going to make it.)  │
└─────────────────────────────────────────────────┘
                      ▼
┌─────────────────────────────────────────────────┐
│   Why? What's the problem? (What's wrong)       │
└─────────────────────────────────────────────────┘
                      ▼
┌─────────────────────────────────────────────────┐
│   There's [a security alert. The airport is     │
│    closed.]                                      │
│   (There's a crash. The motorway is blocked.)   │
│   (Our system is down. We can't access the      │
│    files.)                                       │
│   (Three members of the team are down with      │
│    a virus.)                                     │
│   (My/Our plane is delayed.)                    │
└─────────────────────────────────────────────────┘
                      ▼
┌─────────────────────────────────────────────────┐
│   I'm sorry to hear that.                       │
│   (Are you/they OK?)                            │
│   (How are you/they?)                           │
└─────────────────────────────────────────────────┘
                      ▼
┌─────────────────────────────────────────────────┐
│   I'm/We're/They're fine/not too bad/not good.  │
│   I'm sorry about this.                         │
└─────────────────────────────────────────────────┘
                      ▼
┌─────────────────────────────────────────────────┐
│   That's OK. I can't make it either.            │
│   (Don't worry. We have a problem too.)         │
│                                                  │
│   When do you think you can deliver?            │
│   (When do you think you can make it?)          │
└─────────────────────────────────────────────────┘
                      ▼
┌─────────────────────────────────────────────────┐
│   Could we postpone it [till Wednesday /        │
│    four o'clock]?                               │
│   (I think we have to cancel it.)               │
└─────────────────────────────────────────────────┘
                      ▼
┌─────────────────────────────────────────────────┐
│   OK, keep me informed.                         │
│   (Let me know what's happening.)               │
│   (Call me when you get back to your office.)   │
└─────────────────────────────────────────────────┘
```

5 Application

Focusing on the language you need

Prepare yourself to deal with unexpected events. Working in pairs, practise the following situations. Take it in turns to be **Partner A**.

Partner A: You are travelling to the appointment. Look at Situations 1 to 4.

Partner B: You are in your office. Look at Situations 1 to 4 on page 132.

Partner A's information

Situation 1

Partner B is a key customer. You have a meeting with him/her in his/her office at 10.00. You are stuck in traffic on the motorway. Call Partner B and let him/her know.

Situation 2

Your team is working on a project for Partner B, an important client. You have IT problems and your system is down. The deadline is 12.00 tomorrow. Because of the IT problems you are going to deliver 24 hours late. Call Partner B and postpone the deadline.

Situation 3

You are travelling by plane to another city. You are planning to meet Partner B for lunch – he/she is a colleague. Normally it is a short flight. Today there is a strike and there are long delays. Call Partner B and call off the lunch.

Situation 4

You have a conference call booked for 2.30 with Partner B and a colleague in New York. Your wife/husband is ill and you have to take her/him to hospital. Call Partner B and postpone the call.

e.g. **Situation 1**

I'm calling to see if we can postpone our meeting at 10.

or

Look, I'm sorry but I'm not going to make our meeting.

Language notes

Going to

Affirmative:

I am (I'm) going to be …

He/She/It is (He's/She's/It's) going to be …

We/You/They are (We're/You're/They're) going to be …

e.g. I'm going to phone my office.
We're going to be in New York next week.

Negative:

I am (I'm) not going to be …

He/She/It is (He's/She's/It's) not going to be …

(He/She/It isn't going to be …)

We/You/They are (We're/You're/They're) not going to be …

(We/You/They aren't going to be …)

e.g. I'm not going to be back on Monday.
They aren't going to be ready.

Interrogative:

Am I going to be …?

Is he/she/it going to be …?

Are we/you/they going to be …?

Short answers:

Yes, I am. No, I'm not.

Yes he/she/it is.

No, he/she/it is not (isn't).

Yes, we/you/they are.

No, we/you/they are not (aren't).

Note: affirmative short answers are not shortened.

We say 'Yes, he is' not 'Yes, he's'.

could (in requests)

Interrogative:

Could I/he/she postpone …?

Could we/you/they cancel?

e.g. Could I postpone this appointment?

| Yes, you can. | No, you cannot (can't). |
| Yes, you could. | No, you could not (couldn't). |

Could we cancel the meeting?

| Yes, we can | No, we cannot (can't). |
| Yes, we could. | No, we could not (couldn't). |

too and either

I'm sorry.

I'm sorry **too**.

We have a problem.

We have one **too**.

I like Berlin.

I like it **too**.

I'm not happy about this.

I'm not happy **either**.

I don't like meetings.

I don't like meetings **either**.

I can't make the meeting.

I can't make it **either**.

Phrasal verbs: call off/put off

Notice the word order with these verbs.

Can we put off the meeting?
Can we put the meeting off?

Can we put it off? (not Can we put off it?)

We're going to call off the conference.
We're going to call the conference off.

We're going to call it off (not We're going to call off it).

UNIT 14
Explaining and apologising

Focus

Expressions:
I am (I'm) sorry I missed our appointment yesterday.
I had to take my wife to the doctor.
She has a cough.
I wanted to phone, but I did not (didn't) have your number in my mobile.

Prepare:
…to apologise when your arrangements go wrong, and explain.
If possible, bring related emails to the class.
Refer to the unit Language Summary on page 125.

1 Key dialogues

Overview

Listen to the dialogues (a–d) and answer the questions.

a Why is she sorry?
Did she have a problem with the train?

b What's the problem?
What happened?

c Why did he forget the meeting?
What's wrong with his wife?

d What did he miss?
Did he call?

2 Study points

Check the Language Notes as you do these exercises.

The Past tense

1 Practise the Past tense by writing examples from the table.

forget	meeting/appointment	yesterday
miss	plane/bus	on Monday
have to	finish some work	last Tuesday
have	cough/cold	last week
try	to phone	
lose	address/number	
finish	late	

e.g. *I missed the meeting last Tuesday.*
I had to finish some work.

a ....

b ....

c ....

d ....

In pairs, practise asking questions using your examples.

e.g. – Did you miss the meeting last Tuesday?
– Yes, I did.
– Did you forget it?
– No, I didn't.
– Did you have to finish some work?
– Yes, I did.

Vocabulary

2 Here are some family members. Complete the pairs.

e.g husband ... _wife_...........

a .... daughter

b .... mother

c .... sister

d .... aunt

e grandfather ....

Here are some common ailments. Do you have:

a a cold?
b a cough?
c a headache?
d a sore throat?
e flu?
f toothache?

Now practise exchanges like this:

e.g. – I had to take my wife to the doctor.
  – Oh, I'm sorry. What's wrong with her?
  – She isn't well. She has a sore throat.
  – Oh, dear …

Making apologies

3 a Go round the group and get from each member an arrangement they broke and the reason it happened. Write down the examples.

e.g.1 Maggy was late for the last sales meeting because she had to take her daughter to school.

e.g.2 Faisal missed an appointment with a customer because he had to finish a project for his boss.

b Practise apologising with each member of the group, using the examples.

e.g.1 – I'm sorry I'm late.
  – Don't worry. Are you OK?
  – Yes, I'm fine. I had to take my daughter to school.

e.g.2 – I'm really sorry I missed our appointment.
  – What happened?
  – I'm so sorry. I had to finish some work for my boss, and I'm afraid I forgot. I really apologise.

3 Guided practice

Reasons and explanations

Using the flowchart, practise apologising and explaining. Work in pairs.

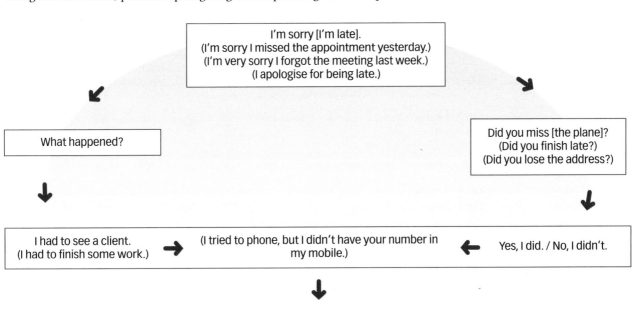

I'm sorry [I'm late].
(I'm sorry I missed the appointment yesterday.)
(I'm very sorry I forgot the meeting last week.)
(I apologise for being late.)

What happened?

Did you miss [the plane]?
(Did you finish late?)
(Did you lose the address?)

I had to see a client.
(I had to finish some work.)

(I tried to phone, but I didn't have your number in my mobile.)

Yes, I did. / No, I didn't.

That's OK. Don't worry.

4 Application

Writing an apology

Work in pairs. Read the emails and decide if the excuses seem true. Then listen and compare the excuses with the facts.

Now think of an arrangement you broke. Write an email apologising and explaining.

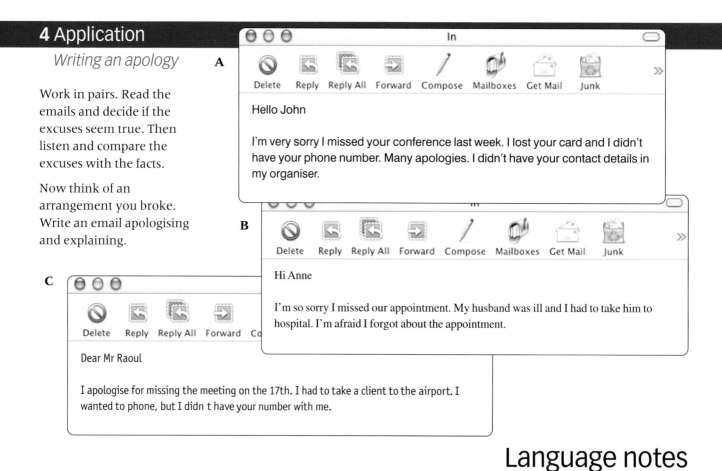

A

Hello John

I'm very sorry I missed your conference last week. I lost your card and I didn't have your phone number. Many apologies. I didn't have your contact details in my organiser.

B

Hi Anne

I'm so sorry I missed our appointment. My husband was ill and I had to take him to hospital. I'm afraid I forgot about the appointment.

C

Dear Mr Raoul

I apologise for missing the meeting on the 17th. I had to take a client to the airport. I wanted to phone, but I didn t have your number with me.

Language notes

The Past tense

Some regular verbs:

call	→	called
finish	→	finished
happen	→	happened
miss	→	missed
try	→	tried
want	→	wanted
work	→	worked

Some irregular verbs:

come	→	came
forget	→	forgot
go	→	went
have	→	had
lose	→	lost
see	→	saw
take	→	took

Affirmative:

I/He/She/It missed …
We/You/They forgot …
e.g. He missed the appointment.
     They forgot the meeting.

Negative:

I/He/She/It did not (didn't) miss …
We/You/They did not (didn't) forget …
e.g. I didn't miss the meeting.
     We didn't forget the appointment.

Interrogative:

Did I/he/she/it miss …?
Did we/you/they forget?
e.g. Did you miss the conference?
     Did she forget the appointment?

Short answers:

Yes, I/he/she/it did.   No, I/he/she/it didn't.
Yes, we/you/they did.   No, we/you/they didn't.
e.g. Did they forget Thursday's meeting?
     Yes, they did. / No, they didn't.

had to

e.g. I'm late because I had to take my son to the hospital.
     We had to finish some work.
     Did you have to work late?
     Yes, we did. / No, we didn't.

Apologies

I am sorry I am very sorry I'm so sorry I am really sorry	we are late we missed the meeting
I apologise I really apologise	for being late for missing the meeting

Focus

Expressions:
Is it possible to speak to Pete Semler?
Can I have extension 401 please?
Is that Mr Semler?
This is Ed Roza from BRAC.

Prepare:
… to make contact by phone.
Who do you call? How do you get through?
If possible, make notes on how your clients answer the phone, and bring them to class.
Refer to the unit Language Summary on page 125.

1 Key dialogues

Overview

Listen to the dialogues (a–d). How well do you think the callers know the person they want to speak to?

i Well.   **ii** Quite well.   **iii** Not at all.

a ....

b ....

c ....

d ....

2 Study points

Check the Language Notes as you do these exercises.

this and *that* *in telephone calls*

1 Fill in the gaps with *this* or *that*. Then practise with a partner.

A: Hello. **a** .... is Tina Krupp from PLK. Is **b** .... the sales department?

B: No, I'm afraid **c** .... is the accounts department. Hold on, I'll put you through to sales.

C: Hello.

A: Good morning. Is **d** .... the sales department?

C: Yes, it is. Can I help you?

A: I hope so. My name's Tina Krupp from PLK. I'd like to know if you sell …

Is it possible …?

2 Rewrite the following using *can/could …?* or *Is it possible …?*

e.g. <u>*Can/could I speak to Mary (please)?*</u>
Is it possible to speak to Mary?

a Could you put me through to Mr Druper?

....

b ....

Is it possible to have extension 123?

c ....

Is it possible for you to hold on?

d Could you call me tomorrow morning?

....

e ....

Is it possible to give her a message?

f Can you give me her mobile number?

....

Using a telephone alphabet

3 In pairs, practise spelling. Make sure you can spell:

- your name
- the name of your company
- your email address.

e.g. This is Ben Ozikis – that's B for Benjamin,
E for Edward, N for Nelly …

3 Guided practice

Making phone calls

In pairs, use the flowchart to practise making telephone calls.

| Hello, can/could I speak to [Derek Ritter]? |
| (Hello, is it possible to speak to ………… ?) |
| (Hello, could you put me through to ………… ?) |
| (Hello, could I have extension 123, please?) |

▼

| Who's calling, please? | ▶ | It's [John Snow]. (My name is [John Snow].) |

▼

| Just a moment, please, I'll put you through. |
| (One moment, please.) |
| (Hold on, please.) |

I'm sorry …
… there's no answer.
Shall I try someone else?
(… his/her extension is
on voicemail. Would you
like to leave a message?)

You're through now.

▼

| Hello. | [Derek Ritter]. |

▼

| No, I'll try again later. |

▼

| Hello, is that [Mr Ritter]? |

▼

| Thank you for calling. |

▼

| Speaking. |

▼

| Hello, [Mr Ritter]. This is [John Snow] from [ABC Ltd]. (Hello, my name's John Snow. I work for ABC Ltd.) I'm calling about ………… . (It's about ………… .) |

▼

| What can I do for you? |

4 Listening

Getting through

Listen to the calls to the Blair Associates switchboard and complete the information about the callers.

a

Name: *Beth Hogan*

Company: ....

In connection with: ....

b

Name: *Roland Lancy*

Company: ....

In connection with: ....

c

Name: *Barbara Lederman*

Company: ....

In connection with: ....

5 Application

Learn by applying

Think about the calls you make and receive. Work in pairs. Practise by making the following telephone call.

Who's calling?

1 **Partner A:** You are the caller.
Partner B: You take the call. Your information is on page 132.

Partner A: • Ask to speak to [Derek Ritter].
• Give your name and company.
• Spell your name and company.

You're through!

2 **Partner A:** You are the caller.
Partner B: You are the person the caller wants to speak to. Your information is on page 132.
Partner A: • Introduce yourself and your company.
• Say why you are calling.

Language notes

A British telephone alphabet

A for Andrew	J for Jack	S for Sugar
B for Benjamin	K for King	T for Tommy
C for Charlie	L for Lucy	U for Uncle
D for David	M for Mary	V for Victory
E for Edward	N for Nelly	W for William
F for Frederick	O for Oliver	X for Xmas
G for George	P for Peter	Y for Yellow
H for Harry	Q for Queenie	Z for Zebra
I for Isaac	R for Robert	

Spelling an email address

Winkelh@kln.com
= w-i-n-k-e-l-h-at-k-l-n-dot-com
All in lower case.

winkelh@kln/sales.com
= w-i-n-k-e-l-h-at-k-l-n-forward slash-sales-dot-com
All in lower case.

winkelh@kln-europe.com
= w-i-n-k-e-l-h-at-k-l-n-dash-europe-dot-com
All in lower case.

Upper case (ABC)
Lower case (abc)

Use of *this/that* in telephoning

This is John Smith.
= It is John Smith.
= My name is John Smith.
= I am John Smith.*

This is DLK Limited.
= It is DLK Limited.
= You are through to DLK Limited.
= We are DLK Limited.*

Is that John Smith?
= Are you John Smith?*

Is that DLK Limited?
= Are you DLK Limited?*

* Not normally used on the phone.

Is it possible to …?

Requests – examples

a Is it possible to speak to Mr Bruint?
Can/Could I speak to Mr Bruint?
Please put me through to Mr Bruint.

b Is it possible to send me the information.
Can/Could you send me the information?
Please send me the information.

Possibility – examples

a Is it possible to change the time?
Can/Could we change the time?

b Is it possible to pay in dollars?
Can/Could we pay in dollars?

UNIT 16
Dealing with incoming calls

Focus

Expressions:
Who is (Who's) calling, please?
She is (She's) away from her desk at the moment.
You are (You're) through to the wrong extension.
I will (I'll) get him to call you.

Prepare:
… to handle the incoming calls you receive.
Do you take calls for other people? What do you say?
Refer to the unit Language Summary on page 126.

1 Key dialogues

Key dialogues

Listen to the dialogues (a–d) and answer the questions.

a Who does he want to speak to?
What's the problem?

b Where is Janet?
How long will Fabio be in the office?

c How many more days is Magda away for?
When is the caller going away?

d What does the caller want?
What is he going to do?

2 Study points

Check the Language Notes as you do these exercises.

who *in questions*

1 Write the questions out correctly.

e.g. (calling/who/is?)

...... *Who is (Who's) calling?* ....
It's John.

a (speak/who/did/to/you?)

....

I spoke to the department manager.

b (this evening/coming/who/is?)

....

Just our two Belgian agents.

c (left/who/briefcase/a/here/yesterday?)

....

I did.

d (is/boss/your/who?)

....

Kathrin Mathys.

e (you/report/do/who/to?)

....

I report to Kathrin Mathys.

for *and* until (till)

2 Fill the gaps in these sentences using *for* and *until* (*till*).

a I am away .... five days.

b Our suppliers will be here .... an hour.

c She will be in a meeting .... 11.15.

d They're going to be here .... 3.15.

e She will be away from her desk .... ten minutes.

f He will be out of the office .... a week.

g They will be at lunch .... 2.30.

h I am on holiday .... 23rd.

Now practise exchanges like this. Work in pairs.

– When will you be back?
– I'm away for five days.
– I'm out of the office …
– I'll call you in five days.

Telling the time

3 Practise telling the time.

i Change the times in the brackets as shown.
ii Practise the dialogue with a partner. (Change the details as necessary.)

A: What time do you leave home in the morning?

B: Normally at **a** (7.15) *a quarter past seven?*

A: And when do you get to work?

B: At about **b** (7.55) .... What about you? Are you still catching the **c** (7.25) .... train?

A: Yes, I have to get up at **d** (6.45) .... to catch it.

B: My wife gets up at **e** (7.05) .... , and my two sons get up at **f** (7.20) ....

A: That's nothing. The baby wakes us up at **g** (5.30) .... every morning!

3 Guided practice

Incoming calls

In pairs, use the flowchart to practise handling incoming calls.

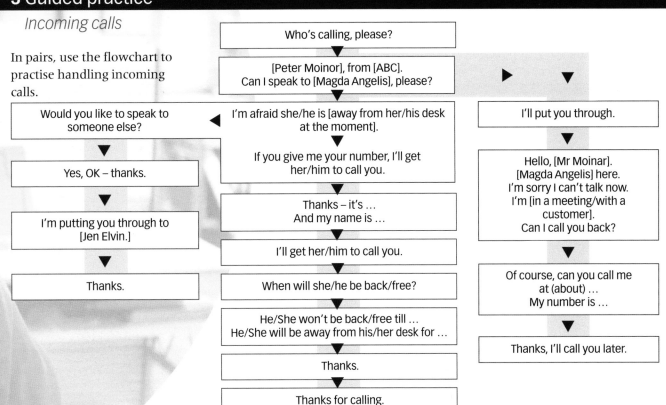

4 Listening

Not getting through

Listen to the recordings and tick ✓ the reason the caller doesn't get through.

Callers	1	2	3	4	5
Away from his/her desk					
On holiday					
Out of the office					
With a customer					
In a meeting					
On voicemail					
At lunch					
Wrong extension					
On the phone					

5 Application

Replying to calls

Make sure you can deal with the incoming calls you receive. Practise the situations you meet in your work. Work in pairs.

Partner A: You are the caller. Your information is below.
Partner B: You receive the calls. Your information is on page 132.
Partner A: • Ask for the person you want.
 • Find out when she/he will be back.
 • If possible, ask to be transferred.
 • Arrange to call at the new time.

e.g. Hello, this is … . Can I speak to …, please?

Language notes

Telling the time

A simple way to tell the time is to say the numbers:

8.15	eight fifteen
9.27	nine twenty-seven
11.30	eleven thirty
7.55	seven fifty-five

You can also tell the time in this way:

a quarter past eight

half past nine

six o'clock

five past seven

twenty to ten

a quarter to eleven

who – examples

Who is (Who's) calling?
Who is (Who's) that?
Who is (Who's) your boss?

Who do you want to speak to?
(not *To whom do you want so speak?*)
Who did you speak to?
(not *To whom did you speak?*)
Who are you waiting for?
(not *For whom are you waiting?*)

until (till) and for – examples

I will be in the meeting until/till a quarter past three.
 = I will not be in the meeting after a quarter past three.

I'm afraid she is away for two days.
 = She is away for a period of days.

UNIT 17
Leaving and taking messages

1 Key dialogues

Overview

Listen to the phone calls (a–d) and correct the messages.

a

> **WHILE YOU WERE OUT**
>
> Call Fernando Ropils on 223897
> after five o'clock.

c

> **WHILE YOU WERE OUT**
>
> Elena Roche will call you before six.

b

> **WHILE YOU WERE OUT**
>
> Call Jan Nagal from Atco tomorrow
> morning.

d

> **WHILE YOU WERE OUT**
>
> Mr Swissom called. Did you get his
> voicemail?

2 Study points

Check the Language Notes as you do these exercises.

ask, say *and* tell *in messages*

1 Fill in the gaps using *ask*, *say* or *tell*.

a Could you .... Peter to call me?

b Could you .... him I'll be late?

c Could you .... I'm leaving now?

d Please .... I'm very sorry.

e Please .... her the good news.

f Please .... her to wait until tomorrow.

g Could you .... her I'll call back later?

h Could you .... her to ring me back?

i Could you .... him for the prices?

Numbers

2 Can you say these numbers?

a 156

b 735

c 11,000

d 5,893

e 109,000

f 259,000,000

g 397m

h 140bn

Money/currencies

3 Can you say these sums of money? Can you write them?

e.g. £550 = *Five hundred and fifty pounds*

a 1¢

b $935

c €1,789

d ¥ 6,586

e 59 Rub

f 1,000 SAR

g 2m Chinese ¥

h 509m Rs

3 Guided practice

Phone messages

In pairs, use the flowchart to practise taking and leaving messages.

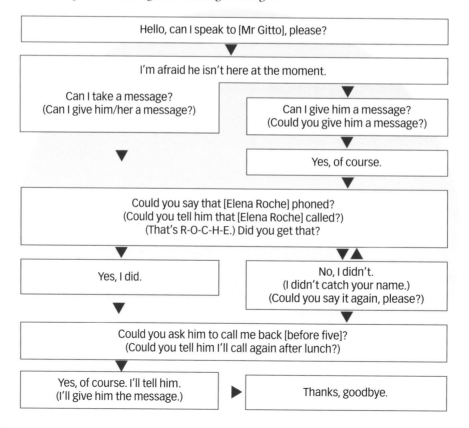

Hello, can I speak to [Mr Gitto], please?

I'm afraid he isn't here at the moment.

Can I take a message?
(Can I give him/her a message?)

Can I give him a message?
(Could you give him a message?)

Yes, of course.

Could you say that [Elena Roche] phoned?
(Could you tell him that [Elena Roche] called?)
(That's R-O-C-H-E.) Did you get that?

Yes, I did.

No, I didn't.
(I didn't catch your name.)
(Could you say it again, please?)

Could you ask him to call me back [before five]?
(Could you tell him I'll call again after lunch?)

Yes, of course. I'll tell him.
(I'll give him the message.)

Thanks, goodbye.

4 Listening
Telephone messages

Listen to the recording and correct these messages.

a Magda called. Could you call her after five? Her number is 7922.

b Call Philippe Buzet on 90876 before Monday.

5 Application
Using what you know

Think of a colleague or customer you need to call. Prepare the message you will leave, then practise in pairs. **Partner B** fills in the message pad below.

Partner A
Can/Could I speak to …?
When will he/she be back?
Can/Could I leave a message?

Can/Could you say …?
Can/Could you tell …?
Can/Could you ask …?

Partner B
He/She isn't here.
Can I take a message?
Would you like to leave a message?

Of course – I'll give him/her the message.

> **WHILE YOU WERE OUT**
> ....
> ....
> ....
> ....

Language notes

Numbers (hundreds, thousands, millions)

102	a/one hundred and two
167	a/one hundred and sixty-seven
300	three hundred
841	eight hundred and forty-one
1,000	a/one thousand
1,500	one thousand five hundred (fifteen hundred)
1,609	one thousand six hundred and nine
16,000	sixteen thousand
125,000	a/one hundred and twenty-five thousand
800,379	eight hundred thousand, three hundred and seventy-nine
1,000,000	a/one million
1,987,876	one million, nine hundred and eighty-seven thousand, eight hundred and seventy-six
245m	two hundred and forty-five million
121bn	a/one hundred and twenty-one billion

Some currencies

$	=	dollar
€	=	euro
MYR	=	Malaysian ringgit
$p	=	pesos
£	=	pound
R	=	rupee
Rub	=	rouble
SAR	=	Saudi riyal
¥	=	yen
Chinese ¥	=	Chinese yuan

ask, *tell* and *say*

ask and *tell* – examples

Ask him to call me.
Tell John to bring the report.
Could you ask him to call me.
Could you tell him to send me a copy.

say and *tell* – examples

Say (that) John Smith phoned.
Tell Eva (that) I received her email.
Could you say (that) I will call later?
Could you tell her (that) I called?

UNIT 18
Email and telephone problems

Focus

Expressions:
I tried to call you at about nine.
I could not (couldn't) get through.
Your extension was on voicemail.
My email bounced back.
Can I check your address?

Prepare:
… to deal with email and telephone problems.
If possible, bring related emails.
Refer to the unit Language Summary on page 126.

1 Key dialogues

Overview

Listen to the phone calls and answer the questions.

a When did Peter Wong call?
Why didn't he get through?

b Where is Igor?
Why is his mobile breaking up?

c What does the caller want?
What is the correct address?

d Why did the caller leave a message?
When did he leave it?

2 Study points

Check the Language Notes as you do these exercises.

try + *infinitive*

1 Write the verbs in brackets in their correct form. Then practise the dialogue with a partner.

A: I **a** .... (try/call) you just after 8.00 this morning about those documents.

B: Sorry. I didn't get to work until 9.30.

A: Then I **b** .... (try) again at about 10.30, but your number was on voicemail.

B: Yes, I had to make a long call to the States. **c** .... (you/try/phone) me at around 1.00?

A: Yes, but I couldn't get through.

B: But you spoke to my secretary.

A: Yes, I **d** .... (try/leave) a message with her, but she doesn't speak English.

B: It's true she doesn't speak much – she **e** .... (try/learn) at the moment.

A: So then I **f** .... (try/send) the documents by fax, but your fax number was engaged!

B: Yes, I'm sorry – there's a fault. Our support people **g** .... (try/fix) it.

Approximate times

2 Rewrite these sentences.

e.g. I tried to call you (from 9.00 till 5.00) yesterday.

I tried to call you all day yesterday.

a I rang you (at 2.57).

.... 3.00.

b Your phone was engaged (from 8.30am till 12.30am).

.... morning.

c I'll send the photos as a pdf file (between 11.50 and 12.10).

.... midday.

d Did you try to call me (between 8.55 and 9.05)?

.... 9.00?

e Could you text me (at 3.03)?

.... 3.00?

f Your phone was out of order (from 9.00 till 5.00).

.... day.

g I tried to go on-line (from 12.30 till 18.00).

.... afternoon.

Vocabulary

3 Match the verbs in Box 1 with the objects in Box 2. In some cases there are several possibilities.

Box 1

to dial	to make	to leave
to use	to send	to access
to open	to delete	to answer
to reply to ✓	to listen to	to save
to forward	to miss	to enter
to press		

Box 2

a phone	a message	a message
a call	a text	an email
a file	an attachment ✓	a voicemail
an address book	a website	a document
an address	a password	a user name
a key		

In pairs, use the expressions to practise asking for advice.

e.g. – I tried to listen to my voicemails but I can't.
What do you think is the problem?
– Why don't you call the help line?
– Good idea. Thanks.

3 Guided practice

Communication difficulties

In pairs, talk about difficulties with emails and telephones using points from the table.

Could you repeat that, please?
(Could you speak up, please?)

I'm sorry, I can't hear you.
It's a bad line.
You're breaking up.

My battery is low.
I'll call you on a land line.

My email bounced back.
Can I check your address?

It's not in my inbox.
Can you resend it, please?

I couldn't get through.
I tried to call you at about 9.00.
Your extension was on voicemail.

Why don't you check your password?
Why don't you call the Help Line?
Call IT support.

Our phone was out of order all morning.
We had problems with our system all day.

I can't access my voicemail.
I can't open the attachment.
I can't log on.

My email address is …
Our website address is …

4 Listening

Common problems

Match the dialogues 1–6 with the telephone and email problems listed below.

a Wrong password ....

b On voicemail ....

c Bad line ....

d Won't open ....

e Not received ....

f Wrong extension ....

5 Application

Solutions and explanations

Make sure you can deal with any email and phone problems you meet. In pairs, write down the common problems. If they aren't on the list, add them. Then in pairs, think of solutions/explanations.

Common problems	Some solutions
Breaking up On voicemail Wrong extension number Can't access mailbox/voicemail Can't get through Battery low	
Email returned/bounced back Can't open attachment Can't log on Email not received.	

Now practise the situations in pairs.

Partner A: You raise a problem.

Partner B: Suggest a solution or explanation.

e.g. – You are breaking up. I can't hear you.
   – Is that better?
   – Yes, but it's a bad line. Why don't you call me when you get back to the office?

Language notes

Some telephone expressions

a bad line/connection
a direct line
an outside line
a land line
a wrong number
a home/work number
an extension number
a fax number
a mobile number
a payphone
voicemail (message)
text (message)
mailbox
enquiries
break up

Some email expressions

email address
inbox
attachment
password
user name
bounce back/return
log on
on-line

try – examples

I tried to call but I couldn't get through.
I tried to email you but it bounced back.
I tried to open the attachment but I couldn't.
I tried to log on but I had the wrong password.
I tried to go online but the system was down

Approximate times – examples

just before/after
– I called you just before 10.

around/at about
– We sent the email around 4 o'clock.

most of the afternoon/morning
– She was on the phone most of the afternoon.

all
– Our email was down all day.

between
– I tried calling between 9 and 9.15, but it went through to voicemail.

for about
– I was on line for about 40 minutes but I couldn't download the information.

web address

www.pod_uk.com/training
= w-w-w-dot-p-o-d-underscore-u-k-dot-com-forward slash-training

See also Language Notes in:
• Unit 15, Spelling an email address

1 Key dialogues

Overview

Listen to the dialogues (a–d) and answer the questions.

a What does she offer the guest?
How does he like his coffee?

b What does the host offer to do?
Which biscuits does he offer?

c Is John's coffee the one with milk?
Does he take sugar?

d Does the guest want a sandwich?
Does she like the cake?

2 Study points

Check the Language Notes as you do these exercises.

Possessive pronouns and whose

1 Complete the sentences using *mine, yours, his, hers, ours* or *theirs*.

e.g. This isn't my cup of coffee.
This cup of coffee isn't ....**mine.**....

a – Is this your briefcase?
– No, it isn't ....

b – Whose cup is this?
– I think it's John's.
– No, I'm sure it isn't ....

c Can we share your sandwiches? We didn't bring
.... with us.

d – Are they your customers?
– No, they're not ....

e – Is that their lorry?
– No, ... is much bigger.

f – Whose are these papers? Are they Rosa's?
– Yes, they're all ....

g – My coffee's cold. How's .... ?
– Mine's fine.

Now, in pairs, practise exchanges like these.

– Whose is this/that card?
– It's mine/Jo's/his.
– Whose are these/those keys?
– They aren't mine. I think they're yours/Anna's/hers.

UNIT 19
Drinks and snacks

Focus

Expressions:
Would you like a cup of coffee?
Can I get you anything else?
Whose coffee is this?
I think this one is mine.

Prepare:
… to offer drinks and snacks.
When do you do this? Where do you do it?
What do you need to say?
If possible, bring a menu from a local sandwich bar to class.
Refer to the unit Language Summary on page 126.

one/ones

2 Complete the exchanges with the phrases in the box.

that one ✓	the one at
the one that leaves	it was one near
one of these	my ones
some clean ones	a weaker one

e.g. This cup of coffee's mine.

...... *That one* ...... is yours.

a This coffee's too strong for me. Can I have .... ?

b Would you like a biscuit? Try ....

c – Which train do you usually catch?

– .... at 4 o'clock.

d – Which hotel do you normally stay in?

– .... the airport.

e – Which restaurant did you go to last night?

– .... the river.

f Excuse me, these plates are dirty. Can we have .... ?

g – Are these your files?

– No, ... are on the table.

something *and* anything

3 Complete the gaps with *something* and *anything*. (Sometimes both are possible.)

a I've got .... I'd like you to try.

b Try this. Does it remind you of .... ?

c There's .... I must say.

d Did you say .... about it?

e No, I didn't say ....

f Are you doing .... tonight?

g I'm not doing .... special.

---

3 Listening

True or false?

Listen to someone offering a visitor refreshments and mark the statements true [T], false [F] or not given [NG].

a The woman offers several kinds of drinks. [T]

b They don't have any soft drinks. [ ]

c They have three kinds of sandwiches. [ ]

d The visitor doesn't like beef sandwiches. [ ]

e The woman has a cheese sandwich. [ ]

f The visitor has black coffee. [ ]

g She doesn't take sugar. [ ]

h She doesn't want a biscuit. [ ]

4 Guided practice
Offering refreshments

In pairs, use this flowchart to practise offering a guest drinks and snacks.

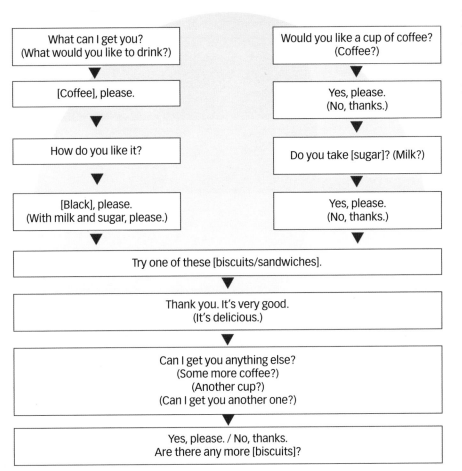

What can I get you?
(What would you like to drink?)
▼
[Coffee], please.
▼
How do you like it?
▼
[Black], please.
(With milk and sugar, please.)

Would you like a cup of coffee?
(Coffee?)
▼
Yes, please.
(No, thanks.)
▼
Do you take [sugar]? (Milk?)
▼
Yes, please.
(No, thanks.)

Try one of these [biscuits/sandwiches].
▼
Thank you. It's very good.
(It's delicious.)
▼
Can I get you anything else?
(Some more coffee?)
(Another cup?)
(Can I get you another one?)
▼
Yes, please. / No, thanks.
Are there any more [biscuits]?

5 Application
Being hospitable

Make sure you can offer a visitor drinks and snacks. If you have local specialities, find out how to offer them in English. Work in pairs. Use the Language Summary on page 126 to help you.

Partner A: You are the host. Your information is below.
Partner B: You are the visitor. Your information is on page 132.

Partner A
1 Offer your visitor something to eat and drink. Make some suggestions (e.g. tea, coffee, biscuits, sandwiches). Ask if your visitor takes milk, cream, sugar, etc.
2 Ask if your visitor would like anything else.

Language notes

Possessive pronouns

mine
his
hers
ours
yours
theirs
e.g. This is my cup.
This cup is mine.

Possessive adjectives

my
his
her
our
your
their
That is your cup.
That cup is yours.

whose – examples

Whose coffee is this? = Whose is this coffee?
(It's mine.)

Whose bags are these? = Whose are these bags?
(They're ours.)

one/ones – examples

This plate is dirty. Here is a clean one.
Would you like a coffee? Yes, a small one, please.
Did you eat all the sandwiches? No, I left the cheese ones.
Which biscuits would you like? The chocolate ones, please.

something and *anything*

Use *something* in affirmative sentences and *anything* in negative sentences.

Affirmative
I want **something** to read.
I'd like **something** to eat.

Negative
I don't want **anything** to read.
I don't want **anything** to eat.

In questions, both *something* and *anything* are common.
e.g. Would you like **something** to eat?
Would you like **anything** to eat?
Are you doing **something** this evening?
Are you doing **anything** this evening?

UNIT 20 Eating out

1 Key dialogues

Overview

Listen to the dialogues (a–e) and answer the questions.

a Would the visitor like to go out for a meal?
Does he like Mexican food?

b What does the waiter recommend?
What do they order?

c Are there any problems with the meal?
What does the waiter do?

d Would he like a large piece of cake?
Do they both want coffee?

e Does the bill include service?
Does it include VAT?

2 Study points

Check the Language Notes as you do these exercises.

Comparative adjectives

1 Rewrite the sentences with comparative forms of these adjectives. Use each word once.

expensive	low	cheap	tasty
good	dry	fresh	bad

e.g. The steak isn't as cheap as the pork.
The steak is *more expensive than the pork.*

a The pork isn't as expensive as the steak.
The steak ....

b The meat isn't as good as the fish.
The fish ....

c The Orvieto isn't as dry as the Muscadet.
The Muscadet ....

d The salmon isn't as fresh as the trout.
The trout ....

e My main course wasn't as good as my starter.
My main course ....

f This restaurant isn't as cheap as that one.
That restaurant ....

g The meat isn't as tasty as the vegetables.
The vegetables ....

h The prices aren't as high in the Indonesian restaurant as in the Thai restaurant.
The prices in the Indonesian restaurant

....

Percentages

2 Write out these examples in full.

a 13.75%

b 17½%

c 65.8%

d 35.93

e 87.5%

f 92.6%

Quantity phrases

3 Rewrite the sentences using the words in the box.

e.g. I'd like some wine.

.... *I'd like a bottle of wine.* ....

a piece	a cup	a can	a glass
a box	a bunch	a bottle ✓	

a Can I have some cake? .... ?

b A coffee, please. ....

c I'd like a Coke. ....

d Could I have some milk? ....

e Shall we give her some chocolates? ....

f No, let's give her some flowers. ....

Then, in pairs, practice exchanges like this.

– Would you like a glass of water?
– Yes, I would – thanks.

3 Listening

Eating out

Look at the menu of the day, then listen to the recording and write down the customer's order.

MENU OF THE DAY

Starters
Seafood salad
Soup of the day (mushroom)

~

Main course
Fillet steak
Salmon in white wine sauce

~

Vegetables or salad
French fries or boiled potatoes

~

Dessert
Fruit
Apple pie
Cheese and biscuits

STARTER: ....
....

MAIN COURSE: ....
....

DESSERT: ....
....

DRINKS: ....
....

4 Guided practice

Ordering a meal

In pairs, use the flowchart to practise ordering a meal.

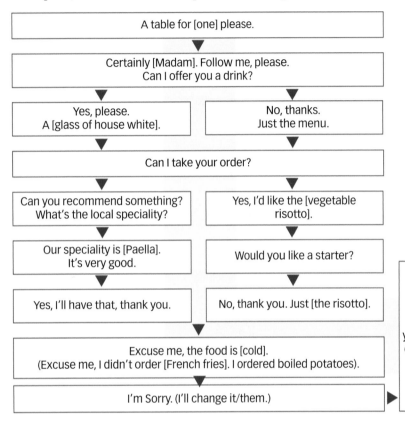

A table for [one] please.

Certainly [Madam]. Follow me, please.
Can I offer you a drink?

Yes, please.
A [glass of house white].

No, thanks.
Just the menu.

Can I take your order?

Can you recommend something?
What's the local speciality?

Yes, I'd like the [vegetable risotto].

Our speciality is [Paella].
It's very good.

Would you like a starter?

Yes, I'll have that, thank you.

No, thank you. Just [the risotto].

Excuse me, the food is [cold].
(Excuse me, I didn't order [French fries]. I ordered boiled potatoes).

I'm Sorry. (I'll change it/them.)

5 Application

Entertaining a guest

Practice the language you need to use when eating out. Work in groups of three.

a Prepare a menu.
b Pass your menu to another group.
c Organise your group so that there are two diners and one waiter.
d Study the menu, then order your meal.
e Start eating and drinking.
f Make a complaint.
g Ask for the bill. Pay.

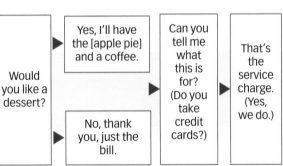

Would you like a dessert?

Yes, I'll have the [apple pie] and a coffee.

No, thank you, just the bill.

Can you tell me what this is for? (Do you take credit cards?)

That's the service charge. (Yes, we do.)

Language notes

The comparative form of adjectives

Regular adjectives

cheap	→	cheaper	wide	→	wider
big	→	bigger	hot	→	hotter
heavy	→	heavier	happy	→	happier
expensive	→	more expensive			
interesting	→	more interesting			

Irregular adjectives

| bad | → | worse | good | → | better |

e.g. The starter was better than the main course.

Quantity phrases

We can say:
- a cup/mug/pot of coffee
- a glass/bottle/carafe/litre of wine
- a piece/slice of cake.

Examples

a piece of cake	a bottle of wine	a cup of coffee
a can of coke	a glass of beer	a box of chocolates
a bunch of flowers	a carton of milk	a litre of petrol

Remember that some nouns are 'countable' – we can count them.

e.g. Do you have a glass?
Do you have two glasses?
Do you have some/any glasses?

Some nouns are 'uncountable' – we measure them.

e.g. Do you have some/any sugar? (not: *a sugar*)
Could I have a bag of sugar?
Could I have two spoons of sugar?

Fractions and percentages

Notice how you say these numbers.

Fractions

$19\frac{1}{4}$ = nineteen and a quarter
$38\frac{1}{2}$ = thirty-eight and a half
$57\frac{3}{4}$ = fifty-seven and three-quarters

Percentages

25.62% = twenty-five point six two per cent
55.5% = fifty-five point five per cent
90.39% = ninety point three nine per cent

UNIT 21
Outings and sightseeing

Focus

Expressions:
Have you been to Barcelona before?
Would you like to go for a drive round?
This is the most interesting part of town.
That is (That's) the oldest part of the factory.

Prepare:
…to give a visitor a tour of where you live.
Think of the places you could visit.
If available, bring printed information about your area such as brochures, leaflets and photographs.
Refer to the unit Language Summary on page 127.

1 Key dialogues

Overview

Listen to the dialogues (a–d) and answer the questions.

a Has she been to Valencia before?
When was she last in Barcelona?
Has she been to the Gaudi Cathedral?

b Does the visitor want to go for a drive?
What kind of festival is it?

c Which building does he point out?
What does she think of it?

d Does the visitor want to see *Tosca*?
Has she seen it before?

2 Study points

Check the Language Notes as you do these exercises.

The Present Perfect tense

1 A man in the oil business is visiting Estonia. He is talking to the manager of his hotel in Tallin. Fill in the gaps in the dialogue using either the Simple Past or Present Perfect tense. Practise the dialogue with a partner.

A: a .... (*be*) to Tallin before?

B: Yes, but it **b** .... (*be*) several years ago. I **c** .... (*not be*) to Estonia since 2002.

A: d .... (*things change*) much since that time?

B: Yes, a lot **e** .... (*change*). Take my company, for example – most of our filling stations now have pay-at-pump facilities. In 2002, we **f** .... (*not have*) any.

A: But I heard you're not building any new ones at the moment?

B: No, we **g** .... (*stop*) building new ones last year. We **h** .... (*not start*) any new projects for nine months.

since *and* for

2 In pairs, ask each other about some of the places you have been. Use *since* or *for* in your answers.
e.g. Have you ever been to [Estonia]?
Yes, but not since (2003).
Yes, but not for (ten years).

Superlative adjectives

3 Practise superlatives by finding out the following.

a Who is the tallest person in the room?

b Who drives the oldest car?

c Who had the biggest lunch yesterday?

d Who knows the cheapest air fare to [New York]?

e Who is the most experienced?

f Who is the most senior?

g Who …?

3 Listening

Inviting a visitor out

Listen to the dialogues. Tick ☑ if the visitor has been to the following events.

The opera ☐

The ballet ☐

A football match ☐

A cricket match ☐

A rugby match ☐

What do they decide to do:
a on Saturday afternoon?
b on Saturday evening?

4 Guided practice

Trips and outings

Using the flowchart, practise talking about trips and outings. Work in pairs.

Have you been/to [London] before?

Yes, I have, but not for ....
(Yes, I have, but not since ....)

No, I haven't. (This is my first visit.)

(Do you have any free time?) Would you like to go for a drive round [the city]?

Thanks, I'd enjoy that.

This is [the most interesting part of town]. (That is the oldest building in town.)
(It's more than 300 years old.)

It's very nice/beautiful/unusual. (That's very interesting.)

What's this?
(What's that place?)

It's ....
I have tickets for .... this evening.
Would you like to come?

Yes, please.
(I've never seen ....)

5 Application

Preparing for reality

Think about what you need to say when taking a visitor on an outing. Practise in pairs.

Partner A: You are the host. Your information is on the right.

Partner B: You are the visitor. Your information is on page 132.

Partner A's information

1 Tell your visitor about your area. Show him or her photographs, pictures from guide books, etc. Point out the most interesting things to see.

2 Ask your visitor what he or she would like to do at the weekend. Suggest, for example, a visit to the theatre or something of local interest.

Language notes

The Present Perfect tense: *to be*

Affirmative:

He/She/It has (He's/She's/It's) been …

I/We/You/They have
(I've/We've/You've/They've) been …

e.g. He's been to Mexico several times.
They've been there before.

Negative:

He/She/It has not (hasn't) been …

I/We/You/They have not (haven't) been …

e.g. She hasn't been to Hong Kong.
They haven't been there either.

Interrogative:

Has he/she/it been …?

Have I/we/you/they been …?

Short answers:

Yes, he/she/it has.   No, he/she/it hasn't.

Yes, I/we/you/they have.

No, I/we/you/they haven't.

e.g. Have you (ever) been to Rome?
Yes, I have./No, I haven't.

since and *for*

Compare:

I've been in this office **since** June.

I've been in this office **for** six months.

I haven't been to Estonia **since** 2003.

I haven't been to Estonia **for** eight years.

The superlative form of adjectives

Regular adjectives

i	cheap	cheapest	old	oldest
	light	lightest	nice	nicest
ii	big	biggest	thin	thinnest
	hot	hottest		
iii	heavy	heaviest	easy	easiest
	happy	happiest	dry	driest
iv	modern	most modern		
	difficult	most difficult		
	interesting	most interesting		

Some irregular adjectives:

good	best
bad	worst
far	furthest

e.g. This restaurant is the cheapest in town.
I think my bag is the lightest.
This book is the most interesting one I've read all year.

UNIT 22
Starting a journey

Focus

Expressions:
Is this the right check-in for Tokyo?
Do I need to clear customs in Tokyo?
How many bags do you have?
Where is the platform for Avignon?
Can I have a single to Milan?

Prepare:
… to go on a journey.
Think about trips you make.
If possible, bring tickets and timetables to class.
Refer to the unit Language Summary on page 127.

1 Key dialogues

Overview

Listen to the dialogues (a–d) and answer the questions.

a Is it the right check-in for Manila?
Does he want a window seat or an aisle seat?

b Does the passenger need to clear customs in Helsinki?
Did she pack her back herself?

c Is he in the wrong seat?
Did he need his bag?

d What ticket does the passenger ask for?
What platform number does the train depart from?

2 Study points

Check the Language Notes as you do these exercises.

to need (to)

1 Complete these sentences using *need*.

e.g. I – departures hall – not – the arrivals hall.
   I need the departures hall.
   I don't need the arrivals hall.

a she – her coat – not – jacket.

....

b I – a single ticket – not – a return.

....

c We – go to Germany – not – go to France.

....

d You – go to Gate 14 – not – go to Gate 13.

....

e I – check in my suitcase – not – check in my briefcase.

....

f I – have something to eat – not – have anything to drink.

....

g We – know the flight time – not – know the gate number.

....

How much? How many?

2 Complete the following questions using *How much?* or *How many?* Then prepare similar questions for your partner, and put them to him/her.

		Your questions	**Possible answers**
e.g.	*How much* .... money do you have on you?	....	Not much. A lot.
	How many .... check-in desks are there?	....	
a	.... time do you spend at work?	....	
b	.... suitcases do you have?	....	Not many. Quite a lot.
c	.... money did you spend yesterday?	....	
d	.... does a passport cost?	....	
e	.... times did you fly last year?	....	
f	.... television do you watch?		
g	.... people work for your company?		

3 Listening

PA announcements

Listen to the travel announcements. Write down the flight and gate number, or the platform number and departure time.

	Flight/platform number	**Gate number/Departure times**
e.g. Finnair to Helsinki	AY345	14
a Eurostar to Gare du Nord	....	....
b British Airways to Bangkok	....	....
c Direct train to Chicago Union Station	....	....
d Japan Airlines to Osaka	....	....

4 Guided practice

Checking in

Using the flowchart, practise checking in at an airport. Work in pairs.

Excuse me, where can I check in? (Where's the check-in desk, please?) (Is this the right check-in for Tokyo?)

You can check in here/over there.

Can I see your ticket, please? Would you like an aisle seat or a window seat? ▶ ....

How many pieces of luggage do you have? Is that your hand luggage? Did you pack your case/bags yourself? ▶ ....

I'm flying to [Sapporo]. Do I need to clear customs in [Tokyo]?

Yes, you do. (No, you can clear customs in Sapporo.) (Have a good flight.) ▶ Is that K3? I think you are in my seat. ▶ I'm not sure. I don't know. (Yes it is – I'm sorry.)

Preparing to travel

Practise the language you need when you are starting a trip.

Listen to someone checking in for a journey and complete the table.

First destination:	....
Final destination:	....
Number of bags:	....
Window or aisle:	....
Gate number:	....
Boarding time:	....

Think about journeys you make by train or plane. List the questions you need to ask, then practise in pairs. Your partner puts the questions to you, and you reply.

Language notes

need

Affirmative:
He/She/It needs …
I/We/You/They need …
e.g. You need to find a bank.
    I need a new suitcase.

Negative:
He/She/It does not (doesn't) need …
I/We/You/They do not (don't) need …
e.g. She doesn't need to phone me today.
    I don't need to buy a new case.

Interrogative:
Does he/she/it need?
Do I/we/you/they need … ?
e.g. Do I need a visa?
    Does she need to buy a new case?

Short answers:

Yes, I/we/you/they do.	No, I/we/you/they don't.
Yes, he/she/it does.	No, he/she/it doesn't.

e.g. Do I need a visa?
    Yes, you do. / No, you don't.

How much?

Interrogative:
How much (more) money do you need?
How much do you need?
How much (more) work is there?
How much is there?

Short answers:

A lot.	Not much.
Quite a lot.	Not very much.

How many?

Interrogative:
How many (more) tickets do you need?
How many do you need?
How many (more) suitcases do you have?
How many do you have?

Short answers:

A lot.	Not many.
Quite a lot.	Not very many.

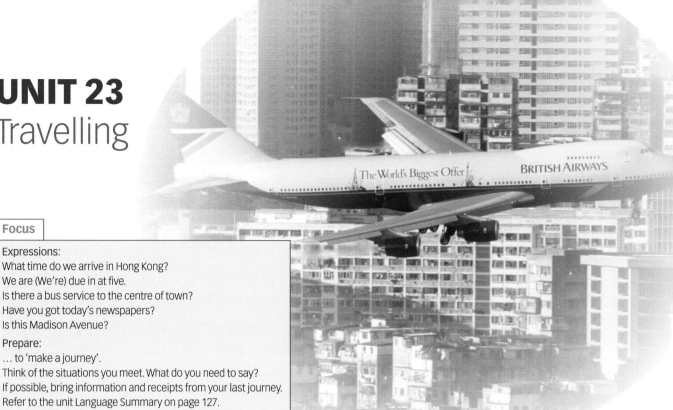

FOCUS

Expressions:
What time do we arrive in Hong Kong?
We are (We're) due in at five.
Is there a bus service to the centre of town?
Have you got today's newspapers?
Is this Madison Avenue?

Prepare:
… to 'make a journey'.
Think of the situations you meet. What do you need to say?
If possible, bring information and receipts from your last journey.
Refer to the unit Language Summary on page 127.

1 Key dialogues

Overview

Listen to the dialogues (a–f) and answer the questions.

a What time are they due into Sydney?
Are they on time?

b Has the flight attendant got today's English papers?
What does he promise to do?

c Is there a problem?
Has he got enough room?

d Are they on time?
When do they expect to land?

e What does the passenger want?
Does the driver agree?

f Where's the bus stop?
How much is the fare into town?

2 Study points

Check the Language Notes as you do these exercises.

Expressions of time/Simple Present tense for future

1 Prepare the questions and the answers below.
Then practise in pairs.

e.g. When/meeting/start	now 3.15 (3.45)	*When does the meeting start?* *It starts in half an hour.*
a When/plane/land?	now 3.15 (3.35)	
b When/train/leave?	now 3.15 (3.30)	
c When/plane/take off?	now 3.15 (4.00)	
d When/we/arrive/Bangkok?	now 3.15 (3.55)	
e When/visitors/arrive?	now 3.15 (4.45)	
f When/you/finish/work?	now 3.15 (5.00)	

have got *and the possessive* 's

2 Complete the sentences.

e.g. Have you got .....*this month's flight*..........

.....*magazine?*...

(this month/flight magazine)

a Have you got .... ?
(yesterday/paper)

b What's on .... ?
(today/menu)

c Could you give me .... ?
(Air Canada/telephone number)

d I need ....
(Air France/number)

e Could you tell me .... ?
(the stewardess/name)

f Can I have .... ?
(next week/programme)

3 Listening

On a plane

Listen to the dialogue between a passenger and a flight attendant, then answer the questions.

a When are they due in to Frankfurt?

b How late are they?

c How much is a mineral water?

d Where does the bus to the city centre stop?

e What is the fare?

4 Guided practice

In transit

Using the flowchart, practise having conversations with a flight attendant or train inspector. Work in pairs.

Excuse me. Can I have [a whisky] please?	▶	Certainly, sir/madam.
How much is that?	▶	It's .... (There's no charge.)
Yes, here it is.	◀	Can I see your ticket/passport please?
(And) have you got today's papers? (Have you got an English paper?)	▶	Yes, we have. (I'll try to find one for you.) (I'm sorry we haven't.)
(And) when do you serve [lunch]?	▶	In [fifteen minutes]. (In quarter of an hour.)
Where's the buffet car?	▶	It's the next carriage along.
(And) what time do we get into [Hong Kong]? (Are we on time?)	▶	We're due in at [5]. (We expect to land at ....)
Is there a bus service to the centre? (Where can I catch the bus?)	▶	There's a bus stop [outside the terminal/train station].
Thank you.	▶	You're welcome.

5 Application

The languages you need

Write a conversation between two passengers using the phrases in Box A and Box B, then practise in pairs.

e.g. **A:** I think that's my seat belt.

B: I'm sorry. This one must be mine.

Think about the journeys you make, and the things you need to say. Then alter the dialogue.

Box A

Passenger A
Are you going to Oslo on business?
Have you been before?
How do you like it?
I think that's my seat belt. ✓
I think we're due in at 7.30, in five hours.
Quite soon, I think.
So am I.
Yes, I love Norway.

Box B

Passenger B
And do you know when we are due in?
Do you know when they serve lunch?
Good. I'm very hungry.
I'm sorry. This one must be mine. ✓
Very much. What about you?
Yes, I am. I'm going to a conference.
Yes, many times.

Language notes

Simple Present Tense for programmes and timetables

What time does your plane leave?
When does the train arrive?
We leave Paris at 10.30 on Saturday.
When does the meeting start?
It doesn't start till after lunch.
They arrive in half an hour.

The Present tense: *have got*
Affirmative:
He/She/It has (He's/She's/It's) got …
I/We/You/They have
(I've/We've/You've/They've) got …
e.g. He's got a good job.
      We've got a factory in Manchester.

Negative:
He/She/It has not (hasn't) got …
I/We/You/They have not (haven't) got …
e.g. She hasn't got a car.
      I haven't got much time.

Interrogative:
Has he/she/it got …?
Have I/we/you/they got …?
e.g. Has Derek got a flat in Brussels?
      Have you got any contacts in Brussels?

Short answers:
Yes, he/she/it has.
No, he/she/it hasn't.
Yes, I/you/we/they have.
No, I/you/we/they haven't.
e.g. Have you got any contacts in Brussels?
      Yes, we have. / No, we haven't.

in with expressions of time
We arrive **in** half an hour.
It starts **in** three-quarters of an hour.
It leaves **in** ten minutes.
Notice these periods of time:
quarter of an hour
half an hour
an hour and a quarter
an hour and three-quarters
a day and a half
a week and a half
a year and a half.

Possessive - *'s*
Next week**'s** timetable
The driver**'s** glasses.
The passenger**'s** bag.
Air India**'s** website.

UNIT 24 Arriving and meeting contacts

Focus

Expressions:
Did you have a good journey?
How was the weather in Lisbon?
It was raining when I left.
Shall we go through your programme?

Prepare:
… to meet a contact.
Think about the people you have to meet.
Where do you meet? Do you go to the airport?
If possible, bring an example of an itinerary to class.
Refer to the unit Language Summary on page 127.

1 Key dialogues

Key dialogues

Listen to the dialogues (a–d) and answer the questions.

a What was the journey like? Where's the car?

b How was the weather when he left Scotland? What was the temperature?

c Why were they getting worried about Marco? What happened to him?

d Why did they have to change the programme?

2 Study points

Check the Language Notes as you do these exercises.

The Past Continuous tense

1 Answer the questions using the words in brackets.

e.g. How was the weather when you left Scotland?

(snow) ..... *It was snowing.* ....

a What were you doing when I called you?
(have lunch) ....

b What were you doing in London yesterday?
(meet customer) ....

c What was the weather like when you went out?
(rain) ....

d What were you doing earlier?
(book a flight) ....

e What was Linda doing when I rang?
(send a fax) ....

f What were you doing when the taxi came?
(pack my bags) ....

g I didn't see you at the airport. Where were you?
(park my car) ....

shall for suggestions

2 Make suggestions using the prompts in the box.

go home	upgrade them
call the waitress	take a taxi
go for a walk	call her
buy one	have a drink ✓

e.g. I'm thirsty. *Shall we have a drink?* ....

a It's getting late. ....

b I need some fresh air. ....

c We need a new dictionary for the office. ....

d It's raining. ....

e These PCs are very old. ....

f I'm ready to order. ....

g Jan is very late. ....

The weather

3 Work in pairs. Describe the weather in the pictures.

Now talk about today's weather, yesterday's weather, last week's weather, etc. What was the weather like during your last holiday? What is it going to be like tomorrow?

3 Listening

Meeting someone at the airport

Listen to the dialogue and mark the statements true [T], false [F] or unclear [U].

a Carita Drago has arrived on a flight from Ros. [ ]

b Janet Riga and Carita Drago have met before. [ ]

c Janet Riga is a company driver. [ ]

d Carita Drago is staying till the weekend. [ ]

4 Guided practice

Meeting a visitor

Using this flowchart, practise meeting someone at the airport. Work in pairs.

| Hello, [John]. Nice to see you again. (Welcome to Lisbon.) | ▶ | Hello. / Hi. (It's nice to be here.) |

How was your journey? (Did you have a good journey?)

| It was very good thanks. | It wasn't very good. (The flight was delayed.) (The plane was late.) |

We were getting worried about you.

Was it raining when you left [Madrid]? How was the weather when you left?

| Yes, it was. (It was raining.) | No, it wasn't. (The sun was shining.) (It was snowing.) |

My car is [just over there/in the car park]. (Can I take your luggage/case?)

| Thank you. | No, it's OK, thanks. |

5 Application

A programme for a visitor

1 Think about visitors to your company, and the companies you visit. Who prepares the programme? How much time is there? Read the dialogue and make changes to the programme on the right.

J: Shall we go through the timetable for Monday? We had to make some changes.

E: OK. Let's have a look.

J: Right, your first appointment is now at a quarter past nine, not at nine o'clock. Joe Staton has cancelled lunch, so we are free at lunchtime. Joe's very busy at the moment – we'll meet him next time you're here. The visit to Gran Ltd is at three o'clock as in your programme, and dinner will be at the Star Hotel at eight o'clock, not at the Reed Hotel.

E: That suits me. I like the Star Hotel.

2 Write a similar programme for a visitor to your company and discuss it with a partner. Make changes if necessary.

MONDAY

09.00	Visit to VCK (suppliers)
12.00	Lunch with Joe Staton
15.00	Visit to Gran Ltd
21.00	Dinner at the Reed Hotel

Language notes

The Past Continuous tense

Affirmative:

I/He/She/It was working …
We/You/They were working …
e.g. I was working in John's office when you called.
  It was snowing when I left.

Negative:

I/He/She/It was not (wasn't) working …
We/You/They were not (weren't) working …
e.g. She wasn't working last week.
  I was working on the report when you called.

Interrogative:

Was I/he/she/it working …?
Were we/you/they working …?
e.g. Was he working last week?
  Were you working on the report?

The weather

Past	Present	Future
It was sunny yesterday.	It's (It is) sunny today.	It's (It is) going to be sunny tomorrow.
It was windy last week.	It's (It is) windy today.	It's (It is) going to be windy next week.
It snowed last year.	It's (It is) snowing today.	It's (It is) going to snow this winter.
It rained at the weekend.	It's (It is) raining now.	It's (It is) going to rain tomorrow evening.

Short answers:

Yes, I/he/she/it was.	No, I/he/she/it wasn't.
Yes, we/you/they were.	No, we/you/they weren't.

e.g. Were you working for KLT when you were in Algeria?
  Yes, I was. / No, I wasn't.

shall

Shall is often used to make suggestions.
e.g. Shall I call you tomorrow?
  Shall we go through the programme?
  When shall we meet?
  Where shall I meet you?

Temperature

What was the temperature like?
It was only 2° (two degrees).
It was 25° (twenty-five degrees).
It was 20°C (twenty degrees centigrade/Celsius).
It was 80°F (eighty degrees Fahrenheit).

Notes: 0°C = 32°F
Fahrenheit is the standard temperature measure in the USA.

UNIT 25
Gifts and saying thank you

Focus

Expressions:
Thank you for showing us round.
We enjoyed it very much.
This is for you.
Thank you. It is (It's) very kind of you.

Prepare:
… to offer and receive gifts.
Think about the times when you give and receive gifts.
If possible, bring thank you letters and emails you sent or received.
Refer to the unit Language Summary on page 128.

1 Key dialogues

Overview

Listen to the dialogues (a–d) and answer the questions.

a Where have they been?
Does he want a lift to the hotel?

b What did the visitor enjoy doing?
What was the weather like?

c Who organised everything?
Why is the visitor so happy?

d What does he ask when he receives the gift?
What does he think of the gift?

2 Study points

Check the Language Notes as you do these exercises.

so/neither

1 Respond to these statements using *so* or *neither*.

e.g. I've never been to Japan.

Neither have I.

a We gave them a calendar last year.

....

b I don't want to go to a night club.

....

c I didn't sleep very well last night.

....

d I'd like to have a beer.

....

e I work for a construction company.

....

f I was very unhappy with their service.

....

g I've never been to Milan.

....

h I'm not coming to work tomorrow.

....

i I enjoy playing tennis.

....

2 Write down five statements about yourself.

e.g. I work for an oil company.
I've never been to Mexico City.
I don't enjoy eating out.

Now work in pairs. Respond to your partner's statements, using *so/neither* where possible.

e.g. – I work for an oil company.
  – So do I.

  – I've never been to Mexico City.
  – Neither have I.

Verb + -ing

3 Fill in the gaps in the sentences with the *-ing* form of one of the verbs.

spend	have	do
play	talk	show
work	visit ✓	smoke

e.g. I enjoy ....*visiting*.... customers.

a I hate .... the filing.

b I dislike .... so much time in the car.

c I don't like .... late.

d I'm not keen on people .... in my office.

e I enjoy .... tennis.

f He never stops .... about work.

g Thank you for .... us round.

h We enjoyed .... you.

3 Listening

Parting

Listen to the dialogue and answer the questions. Note that in some cases the information is not given.

e.g. Was it mainly a business trip?

...*The speakers don't say, but I think so.*...

a How did the visit go?

b Was it well organised?

c Is he coming back next year?

d Why does the visitor give the host a present?

e What is the present?

f Is the visitor travelling alone?

4 Guided practice

Showing appreciation

Using the flowchart, practise saying thank you. Work in pairs.

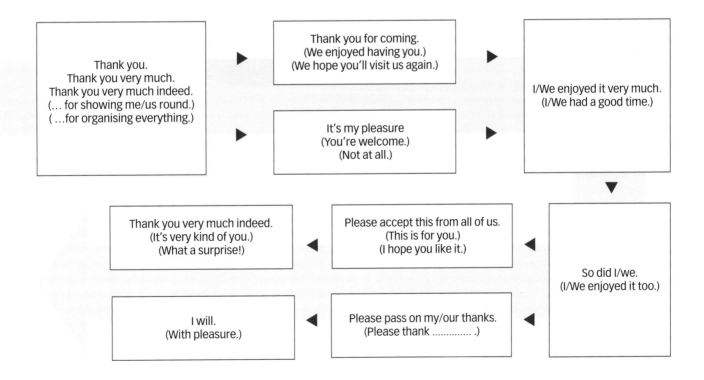

Thank you.
Thank you very much.
Thank you very much indeed.
(… for showing me/us round.)
(…for organising everything.)

Thank you for coming.
(We enjoyed having you.)
(We hope you'll visit us again.)

It's my pleasure
(You're welcome.)
(Not at all.)

I/We enjoyed it very much.
(I/We had a good time.)

Thank you very much indeed.
(It's very kind of you.)
(What a surprise!)

Please accept this from all of us.
(This is for you.)
(I hope you like it.)

So did I/we.
(I/We enjoyed it too.)

I will.
(With pleasure.)

Please pass on my/our thanks.
(Please thank ....)

5 Application

Saying thank you

Think about the situations you meet in your work. Write down the details. Then in pairs or small groups role-play the situations shown in the three photographs – use the details you have prepared. Pick one situation and write a 'thank you' email.

'This is for you.'
'Can I open it?'

'Thank you for everything.'

'Please give this to your MD.'

Subject: Thank you

Dear …

Thanks so much for looking after us so well in Sydney. We very much appreciated the programme you organised. The evening at Mojo's was fantastic! Please, say 'thank you' to Erika. I look forward to seeing you again soon.

Best regards …

Language notes

so and too

I work in an office.		So do I.
	or	I do too.
I enjoyed it very much.		So did I.
	or	I did too.

neither/nor and either

I do not (don't) like driving at night.		Neither do I.
	or	Nor do I.
		I don't either.
I have (I've) never been to Mexico City.		Neither have I.
	or	Nor have I.
	or	I haven't either.

enjoy/like + verb + -ing

Notice these forms:

enjoy	We enjoyed hav*ing* you here.
like	I really like work*ing* here.
love	I love eat*ing* out.
hate	I hate travell*ing*.

UNIT 26
Checking facilities and information

Focus

Expressions:
Is there a scanner I can use?
Is there a beamer we could use?
Which one can I borrow?
Could you print these handouts for me?

Prepare:
… to talk about office facilities.
Think of the facilities you use.
How do you get the information you need?
Refer to the unit Language Summary on page 128.

1 Key dialogues

Key dialogues

Listen to the dialogues (a–d) and answer the questions.

a How do you get an outside line? Where's the scanner?

b What does she want to borrow? Where's the spare flipchart?

c What does she ask him to do? When does she need it?

d What's wrong with his computer? Who can fix it for him?

2 Study points

Check the Language Notes as you do these exercises.

To do something for someone

1 Make questions with *could*, indicating who it is for using the words in brackets.

e.g. (do some typing/me)

Could you do some typing for me?

a (call Roger/me) ....
....

b (send this fax/MD) ....
....

c (give Rosa this/me) ....
....

d (pay the bill/the sales manager) ....
....

e (check the facilities/the presenters) ....
....

f (do some copying/Sebastian) ....
....

g (do something/us) ....
....

h (print this report/shareholders) ....
....

Is there … I could use?

2 Complete the sentences using the words in the box.

e.g. I need to do some photocopying.
...*Is there a copier*............... I could use?

copier ✓	laptop
video camera	computer
room	beamer/projector
someone	somewhere

a I need to do some keying in.

.... I could ask to help?

b I need to talk to some suppliers.

.... I could use?

c I need to record a sales presentation.

.... I could borrow?

d I need to send an email.

.... I could use?

e I need some background information.

.... I could log on?

f We need to check our presentation.

.... we could use?

g I need to download some photographs.

.... I can use?

which, what *and* who

3 Write questions using *which, what* or *who*.

e.g. I stayed with a friend at the weekend.
............*Who did you stay with?*............
Mary Arda. Do you know her?

a I borrowed a video camera from the stores.

.... ?

The Panasonic.

b I took a file from your desk.

.... ?

The one with the red cover.

c I left it with someone at reception.

.... ?

The man behind the desk.

d He gave me a present.

.... ?

A bottle of local vodka.

e .... ?

It was Stolichnaya.

3 Listening

In house/outsourcing

Listen to the dialogue and tick ☑ the jobs they are doing themselves.

a Design of a new company logo. ☐

b Reorganisation of the sales office. ☐

c Installation of new virus protection software. ☐

d Preparation of software for the system. ☐

e Upgrading the data storage. ☐

f Redecorating the reception area and showroom. ☐

4 Guided practice

Some office equipment

a Label the objects in the seminar room.
b Imagine you are using the room for a presentation.
In pairs, use the flowchart to practise asking and
answering questions about equipment.

> Have you got [a beamer] I can borrow?
> (Could I borrow the extension lead?)
> (Could you lend me your video camera?)

> Yes, of course.
> Do you need anything
> else?

> No, I'm sorry, I haven't.
> (I'm sorry, I need it at
> the moment.)

> Yes, is there a [flipchart] I could use?

5 Application

Checking facilities

Make sure you can check what facilities are
available. Work in pairs.

Partner A: You are working in **Partner B's**
company for a couple of weeks.
Your information is below.

Partner B: Your information is on
page 132.

Partner A's information
These are the things you need and things
you need to know. **Partner B** will help you.

1 You need: a room; your own phone.
2 You need to use: a computer with
Internet access; a photocopier; a
conference phone.
3 You need some: paper; files.
4 You need to borrow: a hole punch;
a stapler.
5 You need help with: some keying in.

Language notes

Some requests

We can ask for things using
Can I ...?/Could I ...?/Is there ...?
e.g. **Can I** use your phone?
   Could I use your phone?
   Is there are phone I can/could
   use?

Some examples
Can you have a look at my printer?
Can you send this email for me?
Could I borrow your stapler?
Could you do something for me?
Is there a phone I can use?
Is there a room/seat free?
Is there somewhere I can log on?
Is there anyone who can fix it?

which, what, who – **examples**

He bought a video camera.
What kind of video camera did
he buy?

He borrowed a video camera from
the stores.
Which one did he borrow?

He returned it this morning.
Who did he give it to?

Some office equipment

scanner	screen
shredder	projector/beamer
conference	calculator
phone	extension lead
printer	video camera
fax	DVD player
photocopier	overhead
mousemat	projector (OHP)
flipchart	

UNIT 27 Shopping

1 Key dialogues

Overview

Listen to the dialogues (a–d) and answer the questions.

a What is he looking for?
What is his size?

b Does the assistant have any of the shirts in blue?
Does he have them in a bigger size?

c What does she want to try on?
Do they fit her?

d What does the customer want?
What does the assistant suggest and where can he find it?

2 Study points

Check the Language Notes as you do these exercises.

might *and* may

1 Fill in the gaps with *might/may* or *going to*.

e.g. – I'm not sure if I have enough cash.

– You ...**might**... have to pay by credit card.

a – Do you think these trousers will fit me?

– They .... Try them on.

b – Are you going to offer them a discount?

– I .... It depends on the size of the order.

c – Is your sales manager going with you?

– He's not sure. He .... come, he might not.

d – What are you doing later?

– We .... go shopping. All of us are going.

e – Are you going to Miami on Friday?

– Yes, we .... leave at four o'clock. We already have the tickets.

f – Are you going into the office tomorrow?

– I'm not sure. I .... have to go to Milan.

g – Someone from the bank .... phone. If they do, could you take a message?

h – Someone from the bank .... phone. When they do, could you take a message?

Ages

2 Rewrite these sentences.

a My daughter is sixteen years old.

I have a ....

b This bottle of port is twenty years old.

This is a ....

c This building is three hundred years old.

It is a ....

d The agreement is for five years.

It is a ....

e My contract with the company is for three months.

I have a ....

f The spare parts are guaranteed for two years.

They have a ....

g Our baby is three weeks old.

We have a ....

A newspaper shop

Listen to the recording and write down the prices. How much does the shopper spend?

Soft drinks: .... (each)

Stamps: .... (each)

Newspapers: .... (each)

Keyrings: .... (each)

Films: .... (each)

4 Guided practice

Buying gifts

In pairs, use this flowchart to practise going shopping. There is a table comparing clothing sizes on page 132.

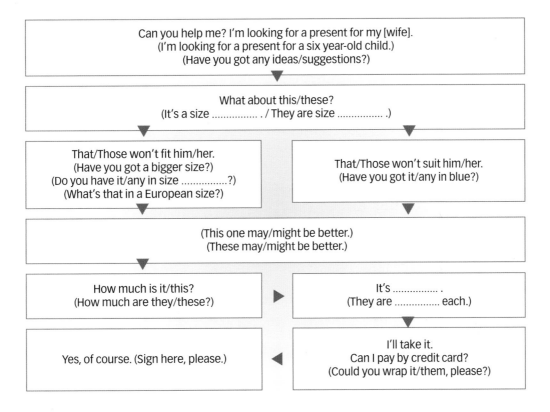

Can you help me? I'm looking for a present for my [wife].
(I'm looking for a present for a six year-old child.)
(Have you got any ideas/suggestions?)

What about this/these?
(It's a size .... / They are size ....)

That/Those won't fit him/her.
(Have you got a bigger size?)
(Do you have it/any in size ....?)
(What's that in a European size?)

That/Those won't suit him/her.
(Have you got it/any in blue?)

(This one may/might be better.)
(These may/might be better.)

How much is it/this?
(How much are they/these?)

It's ....
(They are .... each.)

Yes, of course. (Sign here, please.)

I'll take it.
Can I pay by credit card?
(Could you wrap it/them, please?)

5 Application

A gift shop

Think about the gifts you buy and the language you need. Practise in pairs.

Partner A: You are prepared to spend €50 on gifts for people in your office. You need to buy three gifts. Find out the prices of the gifts in the box and choose some presents. You would like them wrapped.

Partner B: You are the assistant in a souvenir shop. Your information is on pages 132–3.

	Price
35mm films	
Earrings	
Bracelets	
Chocolate	
Sunglasses	
Phrase books	
Guide books	
Key rings	
Postcards	
Local wine	
Local souvenir (toy)	
Silk scarf	

Language notes

might/may

Affirmative:
I/He/She/It/We/You/They might come …
I/He/She/It/We/You/They may come …

Negative:
I/He/She/It/We/You/They might not come …
I/He/She/It/We/You/They may not come …

Short answers:
Are you going to buy a present?
I might. / I may.

In these uses of *may* and *might*, the meaning is almost the same.

may/might and going to

Compare these sentences:
Where are you going to stay?
I'm going to stay at the Hilton.   (definite)
I'm not going to stay there.   (definite)
I might/may stay at the Hilton.   (possible)

Ages

Compare these examples:
That man is thirty years old.   =   He's a thirty year-old (man).
That girl is five years old.   =   She is a five year-old girl.
That contract is for five years.   =   It's a five-year contract.

UNIT 28
Your colleagues

Focus	Expressions:	Prepare:
	Which one is your boss?	… to talk about people who work with you.
	He is (He's) the tall one with glasses.	
	He has (He's) been with the company for ten years.	Think of the conversations you have. What do you need to say in English?
	I do not (don't) think he is married.	If possible, bring photos of colleagues or family to class.
		Refer to the unit Language Summary on page 128.

1 Key dialogues

Overview

Listen to the dialogues (a–d) and answer the questions.

a Which one is her boss?
Is he with his wife?

b Who is the woman in the green dress?
Has she been with the company long?

c Has his new assistant got dark hair?
Is the assistant married?

d How long has the CEO been with the company?
What's he like?

2 Study points

Check the Language Notes as you do these exercises.

How long have you been …?

1 Practise exchanges like these using words from the box.

e.g. – How long has he been in his job?
– (For) about .... /
Since ....
– Has Anya been in the department long?
– Yes, she has. / No, she hasn't.

job	department	company
house	flat	married

ago

2 Practise using *ago* by completing these sentences.

a My manager joined the company .... ago.

b I .... the department .... ago.

c We .... the class .... ago.

d My boss left school .... ago.

e His/Her assistant went to (college) ....

f They (got married) ....

g I visited ....

h I met ....

Describing people

3 a Put the words in the box into groups. (See table opposite.)

b Now, using the vocabulary talk about a colleague and a member of your family. Work in pairs.

e.g. – My sister is tall with glasses. She's got dark hair.
– How old is she? Is she married? etc.

bald	beard	blond	cousin	curly	dark ✓
daughter	divorced	eyes ✓	face	fair	fat
glasses	grey	jacket	long	married ✓	middle-aged
moustache	nose	old ✓	retired	separated	short ✓
single	sister	skirt	slim	son ✓	straight ✓
suit ✓	tall	teeth	tie	wavy	young

Relations	*son*
Marital status	*married*
Clothes	*suit*
Hair type	*straight*
Hair colour	*dark*
Age	*old*
Size	*short*
Features	*eyes*

3 Guided practice

Talking about colleagues

In pairs, use this flowchart to practise talking about colleagues.

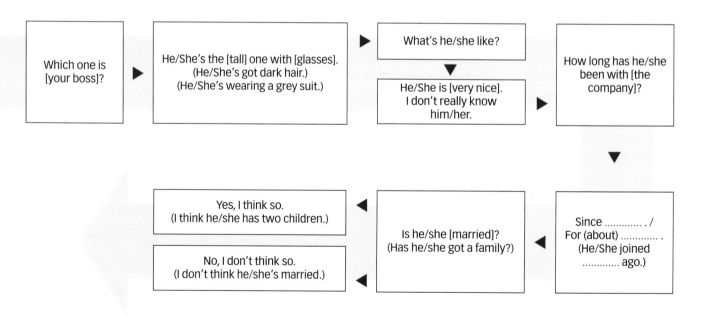

4 Listening

Who is who?

a Listen to the recording. Which people in the group are mentioned? Identify who is mentioned and make notes on what you hear.

b Working with a partner and/or the group, compare notes and fill in the table.

Present

Paul Orhiere (Purchasing Manager)

Nina Luoti (Production Supervisor)

Anke van Breda (Accounts)

Ken Bruger (KC Supplies)

Kitty Hung (KC Supplies)

Name	Job	Started	Comments

5 Application

Your own experience

Practise talking about your colleagues, friends or family. Refer to the photos you brought to class. In pairs, talk about the people in the photos. e.g. This is Caroline Ravich. She is a PA, etc.

Language notes

Language notes

ago

Ago comes at the end of the sentence. It is never used with the Present Perfect.

e.g. I left college ten years ago.

(not *I have left college ten years ago.*)

Stefan joined us three weeks ago.

(not *Stefan has joined us three weeks ago.*)

Describing people

What does he look like?

Size:

He is a tall man.

She is short and heavy.

Features:

She wears glasses.

He has brown eyes and black hair.

Hair:

She has curly brown hair.

He has blond hair/He is blond.

What is he like?

He is very nice.

She is quiet.

She is a good boss.

See also Language Notes in:

• Unit 21, the Perfect present tense

UNIT 29 Your office building

Focus

Expressions:
I am (I'm) looking for the training department.
It is (It's) at the end of the corridor, on the left.
It's not far.
I'm not sure where it is.

Prepare:
… to show someone around your building.
Think about the people who visit your office. What do you show them? What do you say?
If possible, bring a plan of your office to class.
Refer to the unit Language Summary on page 129.

1 Key dialogues

Overview

Listen to the dialogues (a–d) and answer the questions.

a Does Libi Yusri have an appointment?
   Where is Mr Guala's office?

b Is she on the right floor?
   Where is the training department?

c Is the boardroom on the right?
   Can the visitor get through without a swipe card?

d Which room is he looking for?
   Does he know where it is?
   Is he in the wrong building?

2 Study points

Check the Language Notes as you do these exercises.

Prepositions of place

1 Look at the diagram and complete the sentences.

at the top of   at the bottom of
   at the end of   above
by/next to   below   near

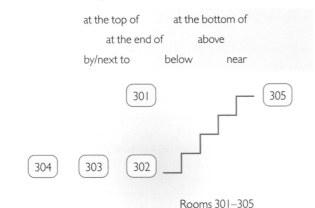

Rooms 301–305

a Room 304 is .... the corridor.

b Room 302 is .... the stairs.

c Room 302 is .... Room 303.

d Room 301 is .... Room 302.

e Room 302 is .... Room 304.

f Room 302 is .... Room 301.

g Room 305 is .... the stairs.

Distance

2 Practise talking about places you know.

The .... is a long way from here.

The .... isn't far (from here/there).

Is the .... far from the .... ?

How far is the .... from here?

It's a long way/It isn't far.

Prepositions of direction

3 Practise giving directions by completing the sentences.

a Go .... reception.

b Walk .... the first floor.

c Go .... the lift.

d Take the lift .... the top floor.

e Walk .... the patio.

f Go .... the double doors.

g Take the lift .... the ground floor.

h Walk .... the building.

3 Listening

Signing in

a Visitors to the Head Office of Univek Ltd (see floor plan below) have to report to Reception. Listen to the two visitors and complete the signing in book.

b Using the recording and the floor plan, identify the number of the room each visitor is going to.

VISITORS' BOOK

Name	Company	Purpose of visit
a	b	c
d	e	f

Univek Ltd.
Head office floor plan

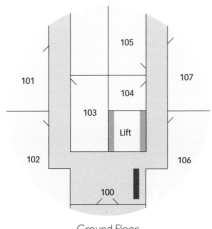

Ground Floor

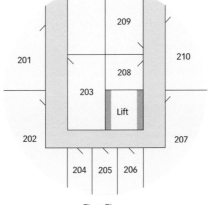

First Floor

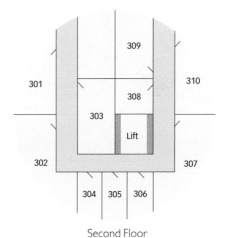

Second Floor

Key

100	Reception	201	Records	301	Catering Dept and Kitchen
101	Data Processing Centre	202	Conference Room A	302	Cafeteria
102	Sales and Marketing	203	Storeroom	303	Medical Unit
103	Postroom	204	Sales Director	304	Secretaries' Office
104	Gentlemen	205	Finance Director	305	Personnel Director
105	Maintenance	206	Managing Director	306	Purchasing Director
106	Purchasing	207	Legal Dept	307	Recruitment
107	Finance and Accounts	208	Ladies	308	Gentlemen
		209	Human Resources (HR)	309	Conference Room B
		210	Boardroom	310	Training and Development

4 Guided practice
Directions in a building

In pairs, use the flowchart to practise finding your way round an office building.

I'm looking for [the training department]?
(Is this the right way for/to .... ?)
(Is the training department on this floor?)

▼   ▼

Take the lift to the [seventh floor].
When you come out of the lift, turn [right].
It's [at the end of the corridor], on the left/right.

I'm afraid you're on the wrong floor.
(It isn't this way.)
(It's in another building.)

▼   ▼

Which floor/building do I need?

▼

Where's the lift?
(Where are the stairs?)

◄

I'm not sure where it is/which floor it's on.
Go back to [the ground floor reception] and ask again.

▼

It's/They're over there.

▼

Can I get through without a swipe card?

▼

Press the green button and someone will open the door.

5 Application
Your own case

Make sure you can give directions round your building. In pairs, use the plan you brought to the class or one you have made. Give your partner a 'tour around the building'.

e.g. The boardroom is down here. My office is the third on the right. The stairs are this way.

Language notes

Prepositions

1 Place
at the end of the corridor
at the top of the stairs
at the bottom of the stairs

at the station   at home
at the bus stop   at work
at the airport   at school

above   below   near   by/next to

2 Direction

out of   into   up to

down to   on to   back to

far, a long way – examples

Affirmative:
A is a long way (from B).
It's a long way (to B).

Negative:
A is not far (from C).
It isn't far (to C)
It isn't a long way (to C).

Interrogative:
Is A far (from D)?
Is it far (to D)?
Is it a long way (to D)?

Short answers:
How far is it?
A long way. / Not far.

UNIT 30
How things work

Focus

Expressions:
Do you know how it works?
First, plug it in. Then …
You switch it on like this.
Does it normally make that noise?
I think there's a problem. I can't access my files.

Prepare:
… to ask or explain how something works.
What do you do if there is a problem? Who do you ask?
Can you explain in English?
Refer to the unit Language Summary on page 129.

1 Key dialogues

Overview

Listen to the dialogues (a–d) and answer the questions.

a How do you start the DVD player?
Is it plugged in?

b Which button do you press to start it?
And to stop it?

c Does he know how to use it?
Where are the instructions?

d Is there a problem with the computer?
What's the problem?

2 Study point

Check the Language Notes as you do these exercises.

Phrasal verbs

1 Look at these examples of phrasal verbs.

It's off/on.   Switch it off/on.   Turn it off/on.
Plug it in.   Put the plug in.   Take the plug out.

Now practise by rewriting the following sentences
as shown.

e.g. Plug in the video recorder.
    Plug it in. .

a Switch on the photocopier.
....

b Switch off the lights.
....

c Turn on the fax machine.
....

d Turn off the computers.
....

e Plug in the machine.
....

f Call off the meeting.
....

g Take the CD out.
....

Simple Passive

2 Write the missing sentences.

a I plugged it in.   *It is plugged in* .

b ....   It is switched on.

c I didn't switch them off.   ....

d ....   They aren't turned on.

e Did you turn it off?   ....

f ....   Are they plugged in?

g We called it off.   ....

Adverbs of frequency

3 Make true statements using the adverbs in the box.

normally	usually	always	often
sometimes	never	hardly ever	ever

a *I sometimes* go to Tokyo.

b .... work on Sunday.

c .... visit the HR department.

d .... speak to my Managing Director.

e .... have lunch with my wife/husband.

f .... take sugar in my coffee.

g .... have vegetarian food.

3 Listening

Trouble shooting

Listen to the recording and tick ✓ the problem.

Fault Log

	Not plugged in	Not switched on	Not charged	Jammed (give details)	Other (give details)
digital camera					
shredder					

4 Guided practice

Equipment that isn't working

In pairs, use the flowchart to practise asking how things work, and offering support.

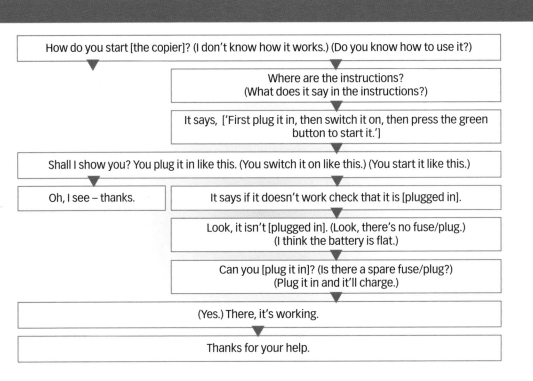

How do you start [the copier]? (I don't know how it works.) (Do you know how to use it?)

Where are the instructions? (What does it say in the instructions?)

It says, ['First plug it in, then switch it on, then press the green button to start it.']

Shall I show you? You plug it in like this. (You switch it on like this.) (You start it like this.)

Oh, I see – thanks.   It says if it doesn't work check that it is [plugged in].

Look, it isn't [plugged in]. (Look, there's no fuse/plug.) (I think the battery is flat.)

Can you [plug it in]? (Is there a spare fuse/plug?) (Plug it in and it'll charge.)

(Yes.) There, it's working.

Thanks for your help.

5 Application

Step by step

Practise talking about how things work.

a Put the following instructions in the right sequence.

[   ]   Put the document here.

[l]   Plug in the copier.

[   ]   Switch on the machine.

[   ]   Switch off the electricity.

[   ]   Check that there is enough paper in the paper-tray.

b Think of equipment you use – for example, your mobile phone or your laptop. Then tell your partner how to use it, step by step.

[   ]   Press the start button.

[   ]   Take out the plug.

[   ]   Select the number of copies.

[   ]   Switch on the electricity.

[   ]   Switch off the machine.

Language notes

The Simple Passive: Present tense

Affirmative:
It is (It's) switched on here.
They are (They're) switched on like this.

Negative:
It is not (isn't) switched on with the red button.
They are not (aren't) switched on at the wall.

Interrogative:
Is it switched on like this?
Are they switched on there?

Short answers:
Yes, it is. / No, it isn't.
Yes, they are. / No, they aren't.

Adverbs of frequency: *How often?*

e.g.   How often do you go to the cinema?
      Do you ever go to the opera?

From **most** to **least often**

I **always** have coffee for breakfast.
I **usually** have a bath in the morning.
I **normally** get to work at 8.30.

I **very often** go away at weekends.
I **often** go out in the evenings.
I **sometimes** go to the cinema.
I don't **often** eat fish.
I don't stay at home **very often**.
I **occasionally** travel to France.
I **hardly** ever get ill.
I **never** play golf.

Position of frequency adverbs:

– With one-part verbs
e.g.   I always have coffee for breakfast.
      (not *I have always* …)
      I very often go abroad for my work.
      (not *I go very* …)

– With two-part verbs
e.g.   She has always been helpful.
      (not *She always* …)
      We were often invited to his house.
      (not *We often* …)

– With am/are/is/was/were
e.g.   She is usually late.
      I am never at home these days.

Sequences

First, do this.
Then do that.
And then do this.
Finally, do that.

Phrasal verbs

Phrasal verbs are verbs made of two words. Sometimes they have an object.

e.g.	**Verb**	**Object**
	Try on	a suit
	Call off	the meeting
	Switch on	the machine

You can say:

try on a suit	**or**	**try** a suit **on**
call off the meeting	**or**	**call** the meeting **off**
switch on the machine	**or**	**switch** the machine **on**

… But *it*, *them*, *me*, *us* (pronouns) always go before *off*, *in*, *on*, etc.

Try it on.
Plug them in.
Switch it off.
Call it off.

UNIT 31 Requesting information

1 Key dialogues

Overview

Listen to the dialogues (a–d) and answer the questions.

a What is the reference number?
What is it made of?

b Is the model number: ELC 901K?
Is it available in grey?

c How big is the desk?
Can they order on-line?

d Do they have the standard model in stock?
What does he order?

2 Study points

Check the Language Notes as you do these exercises.

Measurements of length

1 Practise talking about measurements. Fill in the gaps below.

a 1.25m = ...

b .... = one point four five kilometres

c 1.6km = ...

d 4.75m = ...

e .... = six point three kilometres

f 1.25m × 90cm = ...

g .... = two point six metres by one point five metres

Discussing measurements

2 Discuss the measurements around you.

Questions		Answers
How big is the	room? table? window? door? computer screen? laptop? briefcase? etc.	It's about eight metres by five metres. etc.

Order of adjectives

3 Rewrite the examples, adding two adjectives.

Sizes: *large, big, medium-sized, small*, etc.
Shapes: *round, square, oblong*, etc.
Colours: *blue, green, black, white*, etc.
Composition: *plastic, wooden, metal, leather, melamine*, etc.

e.g. I'd like to order a carpet.

I'd like to order a small, blue carpet.

a Have you got any desks in stock?

....

b I want a swivel chair.

....

c I need a meeting table.

....

d The filing cabinets are out of stock.

....

e Can I order five shelf units?

....

f I'm looking for a table lamp.

....

g Do you have a wall clock?

....

h Is it possible to deliver a meeting table by Friday?

....

3 Listening

Ordering office furniture

Listen to the dialogue and fill in this order form. (Some of the information is not given.)

Order form

Product: ....

Model no.: ....

Size: ....

Colour: ....

No. ordered: ....

Price: ....

Delivery: ....

4 Guided practice

Requesting information

In pairs, use the flowchart to practise requesting information.

Could I have some information on [one of your filing cabinets]? (I'd like some information on [your Superlite table lamp].) I have your brochure here.

Could you give me the [model] number? How can I help you?	▶	It's [KZ/235-A].
It's available in/it comes in [three sizes – large, medium and small]. It's [one metre twenty by forty-five by sixty (centimetres)].	◀	How big is it?
It's available in/It comes in [blue or red].	◀	What colour is it? What colours does it come in?
It's made of [metal].	◀	What is it made of?
It's [€145], [including/not including delivery/post and packing].	◀	How much is it?
Yes, we do. / No we don't. Delivery takes [three days].	◀	Is it in stock? Do you have it in stock? When can you deliver?
Yes, you can. You go to our website. The address is offsupplies dot com. And you click on 'buy online'.	◀	Can I order on-line?

Thanks, I'll/we'll get back to you.

Getting what you need

Make sure you can ask for information about products you need.

1 Practise in pairs.

Partner A: You are looking at the office furniture in the brochure below. Call **Partner B** and request more information.

Partner B: You answer the call. Your information is on 133.

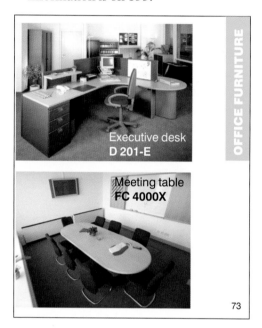

OFFICE FURNITURE

Executive desk
D 201-E

Meeting table
FC 4000X

73

Confirming in writing

2 Read this email confirming an order. Then think about a product you might order and write a similar email.

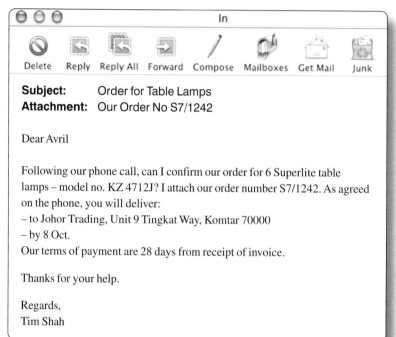

	In
Delete	Reply	Reply All	Forward	Compose	Mailboxes	Get Mail	Junk

Subject: Order for Table Lamps
Attachment: Our Order No S7/1242

Dear Avril

Following our phone call, can I confirm our order for 6 Superlite table lamps – model no. KZ 4712J? I attach our order number S7/1242. As agreed on the phone, you will deliver:
– to Johor Trading, Unit 9 Tingkat Way, Komtar 70000
– by 8 Oct.
Our terms of payment are 28 days from receipt of invoice.

Thanks for your help.

Regards,
Tim Shah

Language notes

Dimensions

How	high	is it?
	long	are they?
	wide	

It is	10 metres	high.
They are	60 centimetres	long.
		wide.

e.g. How long is it?
It's 1.3 metres long and 60 centimetres wide.

Imperial measurements

In some English-speaking countries, people use imperial measurement, especially for length.

inch → inches	1 in = 25.4mm
foot → feet	1 ft = 30.5cm
yard → yards	1 yd = 91cm
mile → miles	1m = 1.61km

Furniture

Carpet	Meeting table
Desk	Shelf unit
Draw unit	Storage cupboard
Filing cabinet	Swivel chair

Equipment

Desk diary	Stapler
Filing tray	Table lamp
Hole punch	Wall planner (annual)
Rubbish bin	Wall clock
Wall clock	Table lamp
Post-it holder	
Stick tape holder	

Order of adjectives

The order of adjectives is usually:

	size	shape	colour	composition	item
a	large	square	blue	plastic	box
a	small	round	black	leather	bag

e.g. a large blue box
a square plastic box
a large square blue box

Focus

Expressions:
I would (I'd) like to book a room, please.
How many nights do you want the room for?
It is (It's) just for tonight.
I am (I'm) afraid we are (we're) full.

Prepare:
… to practise making a hotel reservation.
Do you normally do this yourself? Or does someone do it for you?
If possible, bring emails from hotels and brochures to class.
Refer to the unit Language Summary on page 129.

1 Key dialogues

Overview

Listen to the dialogues (a–d) and answer the questions.

a What does she want?
When does she want it?

b Do they have a reservation?
How many nights do they want to stay?

c What does she want?
Is it possible?

d What is her name?
Does she want a single room or a double?

2 Study points

Check the Language Notes as you do these exercises.

How!/What! *and* so/such

1 Complete the sentences below, using *how/what* or *so/such*.

e.g. <u>How fantastic!</u>   → What a fantastic view!

It's so good!   → (hotel) <u>It's such a good hotel.</u>

a How beautiful!   (room) ....

b ....   It's such a depressing situation.

c How cheap!   (low prices) ....

d (irritating) ....   It's such a nuisance.

e ....   What an incredible deal!

f It's so awful.   (day) ....

g How sad!   (pity) ....

h (We're) ....   It's such a busy time at the moment.

Reflexive pronouns

2 Practise questions from the table in pairs.

   e.g. – Would you like someone
       to carry your bag?
      – No, thanks. I'll carry it myself.

Would you like someone	to carry to wash to clean to park to key in to post to print	your [Mary's] [John's] [your colleague's] [your friend's]	bag? shirt? room? car? report? letters? documents?

Room names

3 a Practise room names by talking about your home. Make a simple plan of your home and then talk about it. Work in pairs.

   e.g. – This is the sitting room.
      – We have a small hall.
      – And here is the door to the kitchen.
      – The bathroom is upstairs.

b Think of a hotel you know and make a simple plan. In pairs, practise exchanges like these.

   e.g. – Where's the dining room?
      – It's on the first floor.
      – Where's the lift?
      – It's along here.

3 Guided practice

Booking a room

In pairs, use the flowchart to practise booking a hotel room.

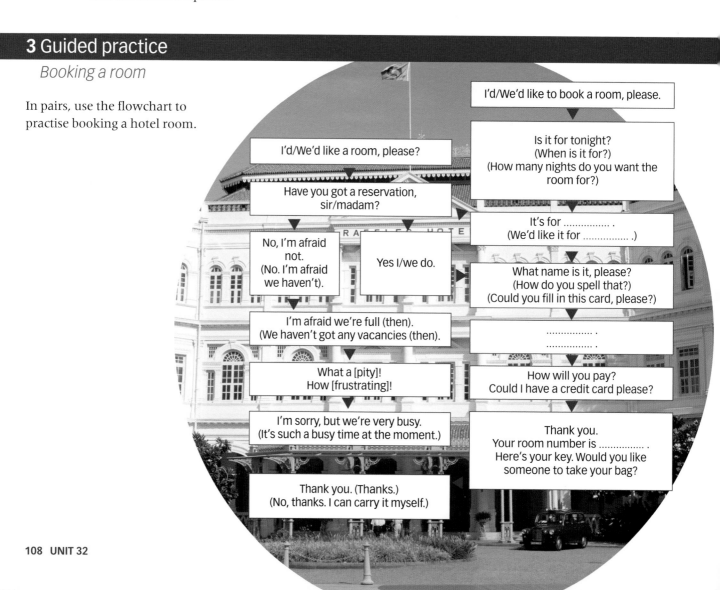

- I'd/We'd like to book a room, please.
- I'd/We'd like a room, please?
- Have you got a reservation, sir/madam?
- Is it for tonight?
  (When is it for?)
  (How many nights do you want the room for?)
- No, I'm afraid not. (No. I'm afraid we haven't).
- Yes I/we do.
- It's for ....
  (We'd like it for ....)
- What name is it, please?
  (How do you spell that?)
  (Could you fill in this card, please?)
- I'm afraid we're full (then). (We haven't got any vacancies (then).
- ....
  ....
- What a [pity]! How [frustrating]!
- How will you pay? Could I have a credit card please?
- I'm sorry, but we're very busy. (It's such a busy time at the moment.)
- Thank you. Your room number is .... Here's your key. Would you like someone to take your bag?
- Thank you. (Thanks.) (No, thanks. I can carry it myself.)

4 Listening

Checking availability

Listen to the telephone calls and fill in the hotel booking sheet.

GRAND HOTEL — **Booking sheet**

Room	4 MON	5 TUE	6 WED	7 THUR	8 FRI	9 SAT	10 SUN	11 MON	12 TUE	13 WED	14 THUR	15 FRI	16 SAT	17 SUN	18 MON	19 TUE	20 WED	21 THUR	22 FRI	23 SAT	24 SUN
Room A (single)		Gud →				Black				→				Smith					→		
Room B (double)	Awai →	Price →							Oliver		→				Rossman		→				
Room C (double)	→		Daniels →					Singhota			→										
Room D (double)	→		Chalk			→				O Brien			→								
Room E (single)					Lucas			→		Barreto							→				
Room F (double)					Loginova			→							→						
Room G (single)	Tane →		Finch		→				Saulnier				→				Jones			→	
Room H (single)			Dibben		→	Thompson			→					Peel			→				

---

5 Application

Your own needs

Practise booking a room in a hotel.

a Look back at the Grand Hotel booking sheet in the previous exercise. In pairs, practise booking a room over the phone.

e.g. – Is that the Grand Hotel?
  – Yes, it is. How can I help you?
  – I'd like to book a room.

b Write an email confirming your booking, using the message on the left as a guide.

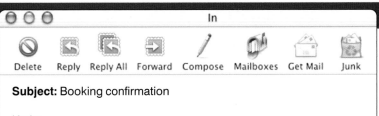

In

Delete | Reply | Reply All | Forward | Compose | Mailboxes | Get Mail | Junk

Subject: Booking confirmation

Karim

I'd like to confirm the bookings I made earlier today. I reserved three double rooms from 10–15 April 20.. in the following names:

Owen Murlagh, Oliver Lees, Amira Baksa.

Their flight arrives at 20.15 on 10 April. Could you please send me your full address and directions from the airport? Does the hotel collect from the airport?

Regards
Sarah Ruse
Administrator
Girdhar Associates

Language notes

Reflexive pronouns

I → myself	it → itself
you → yourself	we → ourselves
he → himself	you → yourselves
She → herself	they → themselves

e.g. Don't worry. I can do it myself.
  If you go to our website, you can make the booking yourself.

Room names

Notice that some compound nouns are one word.
e.g. bathroom, bedroom, boardroom

Some compound nouns can be hyphenated.
e.g. sitting-room, dining-room

Some compound nouns are two words.
e.g. hotel booking, plane ticket, car park

Other areas in a hotel

lobby, hall, landing, balcony, terrace, garage

so and such

It is **so** expensive.
It is **such** an expensive hotel.

We are **so** busy.
It is **such** a busy time.

The booking was **so** late.
It was **such** a late booking.

How …! / What a …!

How beautiful!
What a beautiful view!

How awful!
What an awful room!

How disappointing!
What a pity!

UNIT 33
Booking conference facilities

Focus

Expressions:
We are (We're) looking for a room for a conference.
I think Room A is too small.
Room B is 25 metres long.
When do you want it? All day.

Prepare:
… to practise booking conference facilities.
How big are the rooms? What is included in the price? When do you need the room?
If possible, bring emails and brochures relating to your bookings to class.
Refer to the unit Language Summary on page 129.

1 Key dialogues

Overview

Listen to the dialogues (a–d) and answer the questions.

a When is the conference?
What does he want?

b Is the room big enough?
How much do they charge?

c Is the conference all day?
How big is Conference Room B?

d What's wrong with the Rothschild Room?
Does he book the JP Morgan Suite?

2 Study points

Check the Language Notes as you do these exercises.

Dimensions and measurements

1 Practise talking about measurements.

This room	is (about) 00	metres	long.
This table		centimetres	wide.
This site			high.
My office			
My desk			

e.g. How long is this room?
It's (about) 6 metres long.

Measurements

2 Match the questions with the answers. Then practise in pairs.

a How long is it?	**i** $750 per day	e.g.	– This room is about 30 metres long.
b How wide is it?	**ii** 1.68m		
c How much is it?	**iii** 30m		– How wide is it?
d How big is it?	**iv** 45km		
e How tall is she?	**v** 30m x 25m		– About 15 metres
f How far is it?	**vi** 15m		
g How old is it?	**vii** 14 kilos		
h How heavy is it?	**viii** 28 years		

too *and* not … enough

3 Check the Language Notes, then fill in the gaps using *too* or *not … enough*.

e.g. It's too short. ......*It isn't long enough.*..........

a .... It isn't big enough.

b It's too narrow. ....

c It's too low. ....

d .... It isn't cheap enough?

e .... She isn't well enough?

f It's too cold. ....

g .... It isn't fast enough.

Views and opinions

4 Give opinions using nouns from Box 1 with adjectives from Box 2, using *I think* and *I don't think*.

Box 1

mobile phones	petrol	wages	salaries
prices	taxes	hotels	holidays
working hours	weekends	work	life
television	products	the weather	conference facilities

Box 2

	cheap/expensive	
high/low	long/short	interesting/boring
easy/difficult	good/bad	wet/dry
hot/cold	competitive/uncompetitive	hard/easy

e.g. I think mobile phones are still too expensive.
   I don't think our products are competitive enough.

3 Guided practice

Booking conference facilities

In pairs, use the flowchart to practise booking conference facilities.

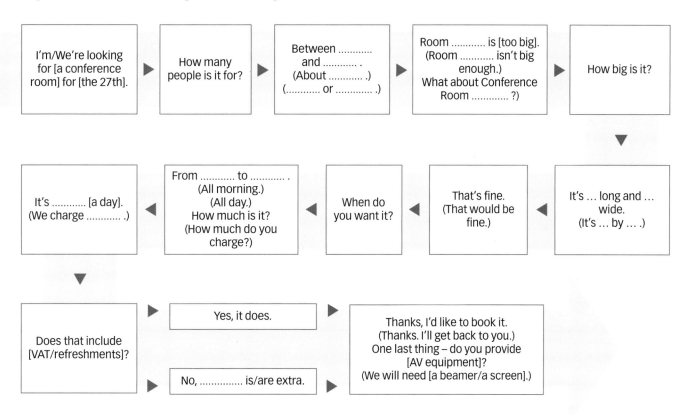

4 Listening

Getting the information?

Listen to the conversations and complete the table.

	Size	Rate	Availability	Facilities
Conference Room A	**a** .... long 15.5m wide	**b** .... per day €1,750 per ½ day €700 per hour	**c** .... this month 4–19 next month	Parking in basement, no charge. AV equipment supplied as required. Tea, coffee and biscuits included. Buffet lunch: **f** .... per head.
Conference Room B	**d** .... long **e** .... wide	€2,000 per day €1,400 per ½ day €550 per hour	1–7 this month 21–28 next month	

5 Application

Your own requirements

Practice booking a hotel room for a meeting. Work in pairs.

Partner A: You are planning an event. Think about the events you attend. Decide what facilities you need. Then call **Partner B**.

Partner B: You are a conference manager at a local hotel. Your information in on page 133.

Language notes

Measurements – examples

How wide is it?
It is 7 metres wide.
How long is it?
It is 12 metres long.
How high is it?
It is 4 metres high.
How tall is he/she?
He/She is 1 metre, 60 centimetres tall.
How old is he/she?
He/she is 27 years old.
How heavy is it?
It weighs 14 kilos.
(not *It is 14 kilos heavy.*)

See also Language Notes in:
• Unit 31, Dimensions and Imperial Measurements

too and *enough* – examples

The room is **too** small.
It is **too** expensive.

It is **too** hot.
They are **too** busy.

This room is not big **enough**.
Are you warm **enough**?
Does she speak English well **enough**?
We have not got **enough** time.
Have you got **enough** money?
Is there **enough** space?

Rates and charges

How much is the room?
How much is it?
How much do you charge?
How much do you charge for the room?

It is €1,000 per day/per hour/per head/per person.
It is €1,000 a day/an hour/a head/a person.
We charge €1,000 per day/per hour/per head/per person.
We charge €1,000 a day/an hour/a head/a person.

What does that include?
It includes VAT.
It does not include lunch.

Does that include dinner?
No, dinner is extra.

Some conference equipment

Telephone conference facilities
Video conference facilities
Screen
Beamer/digital projector
Laser pointer
Flipchart
PA (public address) system
Microphone

UNIT 34 Organising a trip

Focus

Expressions:
I would (I'd) like a return ticket to Bahrain.
I will (I'll) call you when the tickets are ready.
The flight leaves at 09.15.
You could go by train. It would be cheaper.

Prepare:
… to organise a trip, to make plans, to discuss timetables.
Even if you don't do this yourself, you need to know the language.
If possible, bring an itinerary for a trip to class.
Refer to the unit Language Summary on page 130.

1 Key dialogues

Overview

Listen to the dialogues (a–d) and answer the questions.

a What kind of ticket does he want?
When does the flight arrive in Bahrain?

b Is the plane quicker?
Why is the train better?

c When does he want to travel?
How much is going to cost?

d Does the 11.00 flight arrive at 17.40?
Which flight is she going to take?

2 Study points

Check the Language Notes as you do these exercises.

The 24-hour clock

1 Can you say these times? Can you write them in full?

a 09.00 ....
b 08.40 ....
c 17.25 ....
d 18.05 ....
e 05.15 ....
f 20.00 ....
g 14.08 ....
h 13.55 ....

Names of cities and countries

2 Complete this table. Work in pairs or groups.

Cities		Countries	
Moscow	**a**	Poland	**e** ....
b	Bruxelles	**f**	Mumbai
Lisbon	**c**	Sweden	**g** ....
d	Warszawa	**h**	Nihon

e.g. How do you say <u>Moscow</u> in Russian?
How do you spell it?
How do you pronounce it?

when *and* as soon as

3 Write full sentences for the examples below.

e.g. as soon as – we contact you/tickets ready

We will contact you as soon as the tickets are ready.

a when – I arrive in Paris/I call you

....

b as soon as – we make the booking/receive payment

....

c as soon as – we have the details/we email you

....

d when – they arrive/I text you

....

e when – I visit New York/I speak English well enough

....

f as soon as – we pay/receive your invoice

....

g as soon as – I make the call/find the number

....

h when – I get the report/forward it to the team

....

The use of would

4 Practise talking about hypothetical situations. Complete these statements about travelling to work – assume you normally drive.

e.g. Going to work by bicycle *would be much cheaper*.
Walking *would take about an hour*.

a Driving with a friend ....

b It wouldn't be possible to ....

c .... by bus ....

d I would like ....

e Going by taxi ....

f Running to work ....

g It would be better ....

h I wouldn't want ....

3 Listening

An itinerary

Listen to the recording, then fill in the gaps in this itinerary.

Carrier as shown
Check-in time: 1 hour before take off.

		Time	Date	Carrier Flight No.
Depart	London (Heathrow)	10.20	18 June	Continental Airways
Arrive	Manila	13.40	19 June	**a** ....
Depart	Manila	**b**	24 June	**c** ....
Arrive	Djakarta	19.10		CA 320
Depart	Djakarta	09.45	**d**	Trans Pacific
Arrive	Bangkok	12.45		TP 190
Depart	Bangkok	22.30	**e**	Continental Airways
Arrive	London	**f**	1 July	CA 820

4 Guided practice

Booking air tickets

In pairs, use the flowchart to practise booking air tickets.

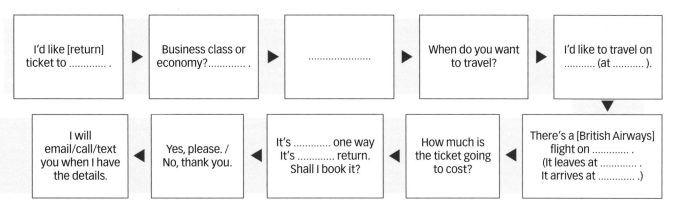

5 Application

Specific needs

Make sure you have the language you need to make your travel arrangements.

London to Berlin	Prices (£)	Journey times
Plane	190 one way 380 return	1 hour 45 mins
Train	102 one way 168 return	12 hours
Bus	73 one way 140 return	16 hours

a Practise by filling the gaps in this dialogue on the right, using the table. Then practise with a partner.

A: How much is it by .... ?

B: .... one way,
.... return.

A: And how long does it take?

B: ....

A: Is there a quicker/cheaper way?

B: You could go by ....,
but it would be ....

A: How much is it by .... ?

B: ....

A: I'll go by ....

B: I'll call you when I have the tickets.

b Think about a trip you might make. Write an email like the one below, telling colleagues where you are going to be.

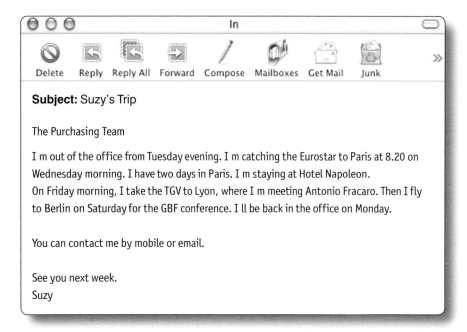

Subject: Suzy's Trip

The Purchasing Team

I m out of the office from Tuesday evening. I m catching the Eurostar to Paris at 8.20 on Wednesday morning. I have two days in Paris. I m staying at Hotel Napoleon.
On Friday morning, I take the TGV to Lyon, where I m meeting Antonio Fracaro. Then I fly to Berlin on Saturday for the GBF conference. I ll be back in the office on Monday.

You can contact me by mobile or email.

See you next week.
Suzy

Language notes

would

Affirmative:
I/He/She/It would (I'd/He'd/She'd) take …
We/You/They would (We'd/You'd/They'd) take …
e.g. I'd take a long time.
They'd take three days.

Negative:
I/He/She/It would not (wouldn't) take …
We/You/They would not (wouldn't) take …
e.g. He wouldn't take very long.
We wouldn't take long.

Interrogative:
Would I/he/she/it take …?
Would we/you/they take …?
e.g. Would you take long?
Would they take long?

Short answers:
Yes, I/he/she/it/ would.
No, I/he/she/it wouldn't.
Yes, we/you/they would.
No, we/you/they wouldn't.
e.g. Would it take long?
Yes, it would. / No, it wouldn't.

The 24-hour clock – examples

08.00	=	oh eight hundred (hours)
	=	eight hundred (hours)
05.15	=	oh five fifteen
	=	five fifteen
07.40	=	oh seven forty
	=	seven forty
16.08	=	sixteen oh eight
17.25	=	seventeen twenty-five
21.00	=	twenty-one hundred (hours)

Simple Present tense for timetables

The train leaves at 12.15 on Monday.
Flight TZ 110 arrives at 16.50.

Simple Present tense for opening and closing hours

The shop opens at half past eight.
The bank closes at 4.30.

When/As soon as – examples

When/As soon as I have the details, I will phone you.
(not *When/As soon as I will have the details …*)

I will phone you when/as soon as I have the details.
(not *… when/as soon as I will have the details.*)

When/As soon as the tickets are ready, I will call you.
(not *When/As soon as the tickets will be ready …*)

I will call you when/as soon as the tickets are ready.
(not *… when/as soon as the tickets will be ready.*)

UNIT 35
Hiring a car

Focus

Expressions:
There is (There's) a car-hire place inside the airport.
What size car do you want?
It is (It's) $450 per week, including tax.
That seems OK.

Prepare:
… to hire a car and talk about cars.
When do you hire a car? When do you talk about your car?
If possible, bring specifications of your car to class.
Refer to the unit Language Summary on page 130.

1 Key dialogues

Overview

Listen to the dialogues (a–d) and answer the questions.

a Where can he hire a car?
What is it going to cost?

b What make is the car?
Is the price OK?

c What is he looking for?
Can he book on-line?

d How long does he want the car for?
Starting when?

2 Study points

Check the Language Notes as you do these exercises.

Non-continuous verbs

1 Complete the sentences using the verbs in the box. (Some of them can be used more than once.)

a I .... to hire a car.

b I (not) .... the red one.

c I .... it's a good car.

d I .... the price is reasonable.

e I (not) .... this form.

f The car .... fine.

g The contract .... OK.

h Their website .... very easy to use.

seem	want	like	know
think	understand	look	

Rates and charges

2 In pairs, practise giving hire and rental rates.

The	rent rental rate charge	for the for my for our for our	car room office apartment	is … per	hour. day. week. month.

That	seems sounds looks	low. cheap. high. reasonable. expensive.

e.g. – The rental for the car is £200 per day.
– That sounds expensive.

Comparison: like/not like

3 Make comparisons using the table. You can update the information by checking the websites.

e.g. – The Ford Fiesta is quite like the Citroen Saxo.

– The VW Golf is very different from the Audi A4.

The Ford Fiesta	is (very/quite) like	the Citroen Saxo.
The VW Golf	is (very/quite) similar to	the Renault Megane.
The Ford Focus	is the same as	the Honda Civic.
The Landrover Freelander	is not like	the VW Passat.
The BMW 5 Series	is (very) different from	the Toyota Corolla Verso.
The Chrysler Cherokee		the Seat Altea.
The Volvo S80		the Nissan Almeira.
The Mercedes S350		the Audi A4.

Car vocabulary

4 In pairs talk about your car and ask about your partner's.

e.g. – We have a Mercedes Vito. It's a people carrier.

– We have four children. What do you drive?

– I have a company car. It's a Citroen C3 hatchback.

– Does your GPS work OK?

3 Listening

Tele booking

Listen to the recording and complete the rental agreement, as far as you can.

Rental agreement

Date of hire: ....   Date of return: ....

Registration no. ....   Make: ....

Model: ....   Year: ....

Colour: ....   Mileage: ....

Tariff (rate): ....

4 Guided practice

Hiring a car

In pairs, use the flowchart to practise hiring a car.

I'd like to hire a car, please.

What size car do you want? When do you want it? How long do you want it for?	▶	(I'm looking for ....) (This Monday.) (Four days.)

That car might suit you. (We have a Ford that might suit you.)

What make is it? (Which [model] is it?)	▶	It's a ....

(That seems OK.) How much is it?	▶	It's .... per day/week.

Does that include [insurance/mileage/VAT]?	▶	It includes ....

(That sounds reasonable.) I'll take it.

Can you fill in this form? (Can you sign here, please?)	▶	(Right./Sure.)

Can I see your [driving licence/passport], please? How would you like to pay? Here are the keys.	▶	(By credit card.) (Here you are.) (Thanks.)

5 Application

Filling in forms

Make sure you can fill in the forms to hire a car. In pairs, go through the form on the right.

Partner A: Your information is on page 133. Question **Partner B** and fill in the form.

Partner B: Answer **Partner A's** questions.

e.g. **Partner A:** What's your name, please? And what's your home address?

CAR RENTALS
25 Stigat Road, London, SE7 8RZ
Tel: 045 258 777 Fax: 045 258 590
VAT no. 200 361 0898

Name: ....

Address: ....

Tel no.: ....

Licence no.: ....

Issued by: ....

In: .... On: ....

Expires: ....

Date of birth: ....

Occupation: ....

Passport No: ....

BILLING INSTRUCTIONS
CREDIT CARD [   ]   CHEQUE [   ]   CASH [   ]

Date ....

Signed .... Signed ....
For and on behalf of Lessor   For and on behalf of Hirer

Language notes

Some non-continuous verbs

Some verbs are not normally used in the continuous.

seem – That seems OK.
(not *That is seeming …*)

sound – That sounds expensive.
(not *That is sounding …*)

look – That looks very good.
(not *That is looking …*)

think – I think your car is ready.
(not *I am thinking …*)

like – He doesn't like automatics.
(not *He isn't liking …*)

understand – We don't understand this form.
(not *We aren't understanding …*)

know – Do you know our web address?
(not *Are you knowing …?*)

Some car vocabulary

Types of car	Features
Saloon	Manual (transmission)
Estate	Automatic (transmission)
Hatchback	Child seat
Four wheel drive	Air-conditioning
People carrier	GPS (global positioning system)
Petrol (engine)	Luggage rack
Diesel (engine)	Central locking

Comparisons: *like, similar to, different to/from* – examples

This model is exactly like that one.	=	This model is the same as that one.
This model is very like that one.	=	This model is very similar to that one.
This model is like that one.	=	This model is similar to that one.
This model is quite like that one.	=	This model is quite similar to that one.
This model is not like that one.	=	This model is different to/from that one.

Rates and charges

Rate
The rate is €4 an hour.
Charge
The charge is €40.
Rent
For flats, offices, buildings, etc.
Rental
For cars, vans, copiers.

See also Language Notes in:

• Unit 33, on rates and charges

UNIT 36
Returning home

Focus

Expressions:
Welcome back. How was your trip?
I needed more time in Lima.
I managed to travel on Sunday instead.
Dick sent you his regards.

Prepare:
… to welcome a colleague back from a trip, and to talk about a trip when you return.
If possible, bring an itinerary of a trip to class.
Refer to the unit Language Summary on page 130.

1 Key dialogues

Overview

Listen to the dialogues (a–e) and answer the questions.

a How was his trip?
When did he get back?

b How is Dick?
What does he think of the new ordering system?

c Did he get any firm orders?
What is the problem?

d When did she fly?
Did she have to pay extra?

e Why did he reschedule?
What did it cost?

2 Study points

Check the Language Notes as you do these exercises.

I'm afraid so/I'm afraid not

1 Answer these questions with *I'm afraid so* or *I'm afraid not*.

a Did you get any firm orders?

....

b Was it possible to change the booking?

....

c Will Joe be available tomorrow afternoon?

....

d Was the plane late?

....

e Is the programme on schedule?

....

f Did you have to pay a supplement?

....

g Was the plane full?

....

instead *and* instead of

2 Make changes to a booking using the details in the box. First, create the booking.

> three o'clock   Monday   business class
> morning   Ocean Air

e.g. – What can I do for you?
  – I'm travelling business class. I'd like to travel first class instead.
or – I'd like to travel first class instead of business class.
  – Can I see your ticket please? …That's no problem.

more (than) *and* less (than)

3 Practise *more* and *less* by giving examples from this table.

Name	Position	Salary	Tax	Paid holiday	Other benefits
Mollie Rana	Area manager	$48,000	35%	4 weeks	$6,000
Gus Bret	Local rep	$32,000	25%	3 weeks	$7,000

e.g. Mollie Rana earns more money.

Reported requests

4 Practise requests and reported requests.

e.g. – Could you come back early?
  – She wants me to come back early.

Requests		
Could Can	you	come back early? upgrade this ticket? photocopy …? cancel [the booking]? change …? make [some coffee]?

Reported requests		
He/she	wants/asked	me to …
They	want/asked	

3 Guided practice

Talking about a trip

In pairs, use this flowchart to practise changing a booking.

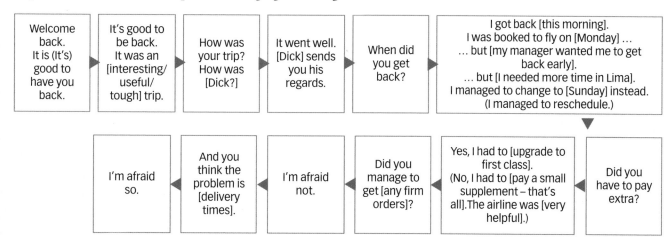

4 Listening

Updating a colleague

Listen to the conversation between Joe Elvin and his boss Jenna Lantos – it takes place just after lunch. Then put the items in the box below in Joe's diary at the best time.

Make calls   Flight back   Print report for meeting

Buy birthday present   Write report   Circulate report

Leave for birthday outing   Meeting with Jenna   Birthday breakfast

Joe's diary	Today	Tomorrow
	8.00	8.00
	9.00	9.00
	10.00	10.00
	11.00	11.00
	12.00	12.00
	1.00	1.00
	2.00	2.00
	3.00	3.00
	4.00	4.00
	5.00	5.00
	6.00	6.00

5 Application

Welcoming someone back

Make sure you can welcome someone back from a business trip, and talk about a trip when you return.

1 In pairs talk about your trips. Where did you go? What were the outcomes etc?

2 Agree the details of a trip you can talk about in the exercise. Then practise in pairs

Partner A: Welcome back **Partner B**. Your information is below.

Partner B: Tell **Partner A** about your trip. Your information is on page 133.

Partner A's information

Using the details you have agreed:

- Welcome **Partner B** back
- Ask about the trip generally
- Ask about specific people
- Ask about flight(s) and changes
- Ask about results/outcomes.

e.g. Welcome back. How was your trip?

Language notes

Instead – examples

We're travelling on Monday instead of Tuesday.
Instead of travelling on Tuesday, we travelled on Monday.
e.g. – Did you travel on Tuesday?
  – No, we travelled on Monday instead.

Sending regards – examples

Their MD sent you his/her regards.
Their MD asked after you.
Their MD asked me to give you his/her (best wishes/regards).
Their MD told me to give you a message …
Tom says hello/hi.

Reported requests

He She You They	wants/wanted asked	me my colleagues the passengers	to come back early. to upgrade to first class. to change the booking. to cancel the ticket. to reschedule. to pay extra.

e.g. (Could you come back early, please?)
    = He/She asked me to come back early.
    (We can change the ticket if you upgrade to first class.)
    = They wanted me to upgrade to first class.

I'm afraid not/I'm afraid so

You didn't get any orders.	→	I'm afraid not.
Did you get any orders?	→	I'm afraid not.
It isn't possible to change the flight.	→	I'm afraid not.
Is it possible to change the flight?	→	I'm afraid not.
You think the problem is delivery times.	→	I'm afraid so.
Is the problem delivery times?	→	I'm afraid so.
It was too late to cancel the ticket.	→	I'm afraid so.
Was it too late to cancel the ticket?	→	I'm afraid so.

Language summaries

UNIT 1 About you

Hello, are you Tom Young?
Yes, I am.   No, I am (I'm) not.

Good morning, my name is Mary Segal.
Good morning. Good afternoon.
Good evening, Mrs Segal.
I work for MAT.
I'm in the finance department.
   Finance   Sales   IT.

What do you do?
I'm an accountant.
   an accountant   an engineer
   a sales rep   a designer

What is (What's) your first name?
What's your number?
It is (It's) 020259366.
   first name   family name
   home number   work number
   mobile number

Where are you from?
I'm from MAT in Hamburg.
Here is my card.

It's nice to meet you. Pleased to meet you.

UNIT 2 About your job

What do you do?
I work for an insurance company called Sarf.
   an insurance company   a bank
   a glass manufacturer   a law firm
How do you spell Sarf?
How do you spell that?
S-A-R-F.

I am (I'm) on the sales side.
I work in the sales department.
   department   division   section
I work in Sales.

I work in the European Sales Team.
I'm (the) assistant manager.
   assistant   deputy
I'm (the) deputy sales director.

Do you like your work?
Yes, I do.   No, I do not (don't).
Yes, I like it very much.

UNIT 3 About where you work

Where do you work?
I work in an office in the centre of town.
   office   factory   warehouse   building

What is (What's) the address?
97 Geneva Road
   Road   Street   Avenue   Drive
It is (It's) near the station.
It's not far from the airport.

There are some good restaurants nearby.
   restaurants   cafes   bars   shops
There are not (aren't) any shops.
Do you have a cafeteria?
Do you have a car park?

We have an excellent cafeteria.
There is (There's) a car park in the basement.
My office is on the first floor.
   first   second   third
We must meet for lunch.
Good idea.

UNIT 4 Your business activities

What does your company do?
We make parts for computers.
We are (We're) in the IT industry.
   make parts   export shoes
   import cars   sell insurance
We're in the insurance business.

What are you working on at the moment?
We're working on a new product.
We're developing a management information system.
We're building a factory in Thailand.
We're opening an office in Russia.

How is (How's) business?
Is business going well?
Yes, it is.   No, it is not (isn't).
We're making a lot of money.

Where are your main markets?
We do a lot of business in Western Europe.
We do no (don't) do much business in the Far East.
We do 90% of our business in South America.

Do you do much business in Eastern Europe?
Yes, quite a lot.   No, not much.

UNIT 5 The location of your company

Where are your company's main offices?
Our head office is in Singapore.
Our engineers' offices are …
   … two kilometres away.
   … five kilometres west of the city.
   … ten kilometres to the south.
   north   south   east   west

Do you have any distributors in Korea?
We have one in the south-west of the country.
   south-west   south-east
   north-west   north-east

Where are your production plants?
They are (They're) not far from Seoul.
Where are they exactly?
They're in Inchon.

It is (It's) a small village. It's a big city.
   city   town   village   place
Is it far from Pusan?

It's about 300 kilometres away.
It's about 300 kilometres from Pusan.

UNIT 6 The layout of your company

Can you sign in please?
This is your visitor's pass.

The main building is that way.
This place is a warehouse.
The sales department is through those doors.
    this   that   these   those

Where is (Where's) the service centre?
It is (It's) over there.
It's behind the main block.
It's next to the sales department.
The entrance is opposite the showroom.

How do I find it?
Go down here.   Drive up there.
Walk along this road.
It's on the left.
    road   corridor
    left   right   straight on

The toilet is that way.
It's upstairs.
    upstairs   downstairs
It's the second door on the right.

UNIT 7 Meeting and welcoming

Good morning, my name is Bill Smith.
Welcome to KPG.
I would (I'd) like to welcome you to KPG.
    Good morning   Good afternoon   Good evening

How was your trip?
    trip   journey   flight
It was fine.
Oh, good.
It was terrible.
Oh, dear.
Was the plane on time?
    early   late   on time
Were the arrangements OK?
Yes, they were.   No, they were not (weren't).

This is Fran Cotton, our PR Manager,
How do your do?
Pleased to meet you.
Nice to meet you.
Nice to meet you, too.

I am (I'm) from France. I'm French.
I speak a little English.
I know a few words.

UNIT 8 The first two minutes

How are you? How is the family?
Fine.   Not too bad.
We are (We're) (all) fine.

How is (How's) business?
Is it going well?
It is (It's) going very well.

Is this your first visit to the States?
How do you like New York?
I really like it.
It's very interesting.

How long are you here for?
I am (I'm) here for five days.

When are you leaving?
I hear you are (you're) leaving tomorrow morning.
No, I'm leaving tomorrow evening.

What are you doing this afternoon?
I'm meeting our distributor.
Are you doing anything on Monday evening?
Yes, I am.   No, I'm not.

It's nice to talk to you.
It's nice to talk to you too.

Have a good stay.
Enjoy your stay.

UNIT 9 Partings and thanks

Many thanks for your help.
Thank you for everything.
It is (It's) my pleasure.   Not at all.
No problem.   You are (You're) welcome.

Call me on Monday.
I will.

Do not (Don't) forget to send those figures.
I (will not) won't.
I will (I'll) email you next week.
    week   month   year
I'll see you in the spring.
    spring   summer   autumn   winter
    at Christmas   in the New Year
    in January   in February
We'll see you in February.
Give my regards to your MD.
Remember me to your wife.
I will.

You must visit us again soon.
And you must come and see us.
See you soon.
See you. Keep in touch.
Goodbye. Bye.

UNIT 10 Setting up a meeting

What is (What's) the date?
It is (It's) April the 25th.

Are you free today?
How about tomorrow?
Is the morning OK?
Can we meet in the evening?
    morning   afternoon   evening

Can you make Friday?
Can you make the meeting on Friday?
    meeting   appointment   conference
Yes, I can.   No, I cannot (can't).

I am (I'm) afraid I can't make it.
I'm afraid I can't make the 26th.

I can't make it till the 27th.
I can't make it till 3.30 on the 27th.
OK, let us (let's) meet on the 27th.

I will (I'll) see you …
    … at four o'clock.
    … in the afternoon.
    … on Saturday.
    … on April the 27th.

That is (That's) fine.
See you then.

UNIT 11 Confirming arrangements

I am (I'm) calling about our arrangement.
I'm calling to confirm Tuesday's meeting.

| calling | phoning | writing |
| meeting | arrangement | plan |

Can I check the day?

| the day | the time |
| the place | the details |

Can I check the details?
Go ahead.

Is it at 9am or 9pm?
It is (It's) at 9am.
Is that right?
Yes, that is (that's) right.

Are you still OK for Monday?
We are (We're) meeting for lunch.
Is that still OK?

Do you know when it is (yet)?
Do you know where it is (yet)?
Do you know if you can make it (yet)?
Could you let me know?

Thanks for reminding me.

UNIT 12 Changing plans

I am (I'm) afraid, we will (we'll) have to …
    … change the room.
    … start earlier.
    earlier   later

Can we change the time of the meeting?
Can we change it to next week?

| this week | next week |
| this month | next month |

Why? What is (What's) the problem?
Why do you want to change it?
Because the conference room is booked.
    booked   reserved   occupied

Can we have the meeting in your office?
Why don't we meet in the afternoon?
Will the room be free by two o'clock?
I will (I'll) find out.

I cannot (can't) make it then.
I have to meet a client.
I will not (won't) be back by two.
Will you be back before six?
    before six   after seven
Yes, I will.   No, I won't.

OK, let us (let's) meet at 7.30.

UNIT 13 Dealing with the unexpected

I am (I'm) calling about the meeting.
Could we postpone it?
I'm calling to ask if we could put it off.
    postpone   put off
    cancel   call off

Why? What is (What's) the problem?
What's wrong?

There is (There's) a security alert. The airport is closed.
There's a crash. The motorway is blocked.
Our system is down. We cannot (can't) access the files.
Three members of the team are down with a virus.
My plane is delayed.
I'm afraid, I'm not going to make it.

I'm sorry to hear that.
When do you think you can deliver?
When do you think you can make it?

Could we postpone the meeting till Wednesday?
I think we have to cancel it.
I'm sorry about this.

That's OK. Don't worry.
I can't make it either.
We have a problem, too.

I will (I'll) call you when I get back to my office.

UNIT 14 Explaining and apologising

I am (I'm) sorry …
    … I'm late.
    … I forgot our appointment yesterday.
    … I missed the meeting.
I apologise for missing the meeting.

What happened?
I had to see a client.
I had to finish some work.
I had to take my wife to the doctor.
    husband   wife
    son   daughter

What is (What's) wrong with her?
She is not (isn't) well.
She has a cold.
    cold   cough   sore throat

Did you miss the plane?
Did you have a problem with the train?
Did the meeting finish late?
Did you lose the address?
Yes, I did.   No, I did not (didn't).

I wanted to phone, but I didn't have your number in my address book.
    in my mobile   in my address book
    your number   your contact details
Don't worry.   That is (That's) OK.

UNIT 15 Making contact by phone

Is it possible to speak to Mr Semler?
Can I have extension 123, please?
Could you put me through to Anna Choi, please?
Just a moment, please.   Hold on, please.

One moment, please.
You are (You're) through now.

Who is (Who's) calling, please?
Can I have your name, please?
Yes, this is John Brown from CTG.
How do you spell that?
Brown; that's B-R-O-W-N.
Could you repeat that, please?

Is that Mr Semler?
Speaking.
This is Ed Roza from BRAC.
Good morning, Mr Roza.
Thank you for calling.
I am (I'm) calling about the meeting.
It is (It's) about the review meeting.

Hello, is that Peter?
No, this is Hans.
Hello, Hans. It's John here.
Hello, John.
What can I do for you?

UNIT 16 Dealing with incoming calls

Who is (who's) calling?
It's Ted Black.
Can I speak to Mrs Martinez?
I am (I'm) afraid she is (she's) away from her desk
at the moment.
She's at lunch.
She will (She'll) be away until Tuesday.
She'll be away for a week.

You are (You're) through to the wrong extension.
You need extension 417.
Hold on, I will (I'll) transfer you.

Can you call back later?
Can he call you back later?
Can I take a message?
No, thank you. I'll call back.

I'm sorry, I cannot (can't) talk now.
I'm with a customer.
I'm driving.

Could you call me …
… at 3.15 (a quarter past three)?
… at 3.30 (half past three)?
… at 3.45 (a quarter to four)?
Do you have my mobile number?
I'm on extension 3456.

UNIT 17 Leaving and taking messages

Can I leave a message?
Could you say that Mrs Gitto phoned?
Yes, of course. I will (I'll) tell him.

Mr Sato is not (isn't) here at the moment.
Can I take a message?
Could you tell him (that) Mr Gibril called?
Could you say (that) Mr Gibril rang?
Please tell him (that) I rang.
Please tell him (that) the price will be $550.

| 195 euros | 4000 yen |
| 786 million dollars | 235 billion yuan |

Did you get that?
Yes, I did.   No, I did not (didn't).
No, I am (I'm) sorry. I didn't catch that.
Could you say that again, please?

Could you ask her to call me back before five?
Could you tell him to bring the report?

I sent her an email.
   an email   a text
I wanted to check she received it.

UNIT 18 Email and telephone problems

I am (I'm) sorry I cannot (can't) hear you.
It is (It's) a bad line.
You are (You're) breaking up.

My battery is low.
I will (I'll) call you on a land line.
I can't access my voicemail.

Could you repeat that, please?
Could you speak up, please?
Can I put you on hold?
Yes, of course.   Certainly.

I could not (couldn't) get through.
I tried to call you at about nine.
Your extension was on voicemail.
   at about nine   at around ten
   just before eleven   just after twelve

I can't log on.
My email bounced back.
Can I check your address?

It's not in my inbox.
Can you resend it, please?
Why don't you check your password?

Our phone was out of order.
We had problems with our system …
   … all morning.
   … all day.

UNIT 19 Drinks and snacks

What can I get you?
What would you like to have?
   to have to drink   to have to eat
Coffee or tea?
Do you take milk?

Would you like a cup of coffee?
How do you like it?
Black?   White?   Milk?   Cream?
Do you take sugar?

Whose coffee is this?
Is that your coffee?
I think that one is (one's) mine.
This one's yours.

Can I get you anything else?
Is there any more coffee?
No, I'm afraid there is not (isn't).

Some more coffee?　　No, thanks.
Another cup?　　Yes, please.

Try one of these.
Thank you.
　　a sandwich　　a biscuit　　a cake
It is (It's) very good.
It's delicious.

UNIT 20 Eating out

Do you like fish?
　　fish　　steak　　chicken　　vegetarian food
I do not (don't) like steak very much.

I know a very good Chinese restaurant.
　　Indian　　Thai　　French　　Indonesian
Would you like to go there this evening?

Excuse me, can we have the menu, please?
Could you tell me what this is?
What do you recommend?
I will (I'll) have the beef.
　　the beef　　the pork
　　the veal　　the salmon
And we would (we'd) like a bottle of house red.

Enjoy your meal!
Cheers!

This food is cold.
I didn't order this.
I'm sorry, I'll change it.

Can I have the bill please?
Does the bill include service?
It includes tax at 17½ per cent, but not service.

The starter was better than the main course.
　　better　　worse　　cheaper　　more expensive
The dessert was not (wasn't) as good as the main course.

UNIT 21 Outings and sightseeing

Have you been here before?
　　Yes, I have.　　No, I have not (haven't).
Have you ever been to Athens?
I haven't been there for many years.
I haven't been there since 2002.

Do you have any free time this afternoon?
Would you like to go for a drive round the city?
　　the city　　the village　　the area
Thanks. I would (I'd) enjoy that.

This is the most interesting part of town.
That building is more than 300 years old.
It is (It's) the oldest building in the town.
　　oldest　　most beautiful　　most unusual

That is (That's) the new leisure centre.
　　leisure centre　　town hall
　　church　　shopping centre
It's the most modern building here.

I have (I've) got some tickets for the opera.
　　the opera　　the cinema
　　the theatre　　a football match
Would you like to come?

UNIT 22 Starting a journey

Excuse me, which platform do I need for Avignon?
Is this the right platform for Avignon?
You need platform six.

Can I check in?
Is this the right check-in for Tokyo?
Where is the check-in desk?

Can I see your ticket, please?
Can I see your passport, please?
Can I have an aisle seat?
　　an aisle seat? a window seat?
This is your boarding card.

I am (I'm) flying to Los Angeles.
Do I need to clear customs in Dallas?
No, you can clear customs in Los Angeles.

How many pieces of luggage do you have?
Just two pieces.
Is that your hand luggage?
Did you pack your cases yourself?

I think you are (you're) in the wrong seat.
This seat is A5.
I'm sorry.
No problem.

UNIT 23 Travelling

What time do we get into Hong Kong?
We are (We're) due in at five.
We expect to land in twenty minutes.
Are we on time?

When do you serve lunch?
In three-quarters of an hour.
　　in a quarter of an hour　　in half an hour
　　in fifteen minutes　　in thirty minutes

Is there a bus service to the centre?
Where can I catch the bus?
There is (There's) a bus stop outside the terminal.
Just follow the signs.
How much is the fare?

Have you got this month's magazine?
Have you got today's newspaper?
I am (I'm) sorry we have not (haven't).
I will (I'll) try and find one for you.

Can I have a whisky, please?
How much is that?
It is (It's) three dollars.
Thank you.

UNIT 24 Arriving and meeting contacts

Hello, it is (it's) good to see you again.
Did you have a good journey?
Yes, very good, thanks.

How was the journey?
It was not (wasn't) very good.
The flight was delayed.
The plane was late.
We were getting worried about you.

How was the weather when you left?
It was beautiful.
    very nice   terrible   awful
It was 20° (twenty degrees).

It was snowing.
The sun was shining.
Was it raining when you left?
Yes, it was.   No, it wasn't.

My car is just over there.
Can I take your luggage?

Shall we go through your programme?
    programme   timetable   itinerary   schedule
We had to make some changes.
Your first appointment is now at ten o'clock.
That suits me.

UNIT 25 Gifts and saying thank you

Many thanks for showing me round.
It is (It's) my pleasure.
You are (you're) welcome.
I enjoyed it very much.
So did I.
I am (I'm) afraid I did not (didn't) enjoy it (very much).
Neither did I.

Thank you …
    … for everything.
    … for looking after us.
We had a very good time.
Please pass on my thanks.
Say 'thank you' to Mary.

Thank you for coming.
We enjoyed having you.
We hope you will come and visit us again.
We look forward to seeing you again soon.

Please accept this gift from all of us.
I hope you like it.
This is for you.

It's wonderful. Thank you.
Thank you very much indeed.
It's very kind of you.
What a surprise!

UNIT 26 Checking facilities

Can I use your phone?
Is there a phone I can use?
    a fax machine   a scanner
    a computer   a projector

What kind of system have you got?

Could I borrow a video recorder?
    an extension lead   a flipchart

Which one can I use?

Could you lend me your pen?
    pen   hole punch   stapler
Yes, of course.
Sorry, I need it at the moment.

Is there a room free?
is there a room available?

Is there a room I could use?
Is there a place I could work?
    have a meeting   do some photocopying

Could you do something for me?
Could you do some typing for me?
Could you do it for me?

Could you have a look at my computer?
There is (There's) something wrong with it.

UNIT 27 Shopping

Can you help me?
I am (I'm) looking for a present …
    … for my wife.
    … for my husband.
    … for a six year-old child.
My son is six years old.
Have you got any ideas?

I like this.
How much is it?
How much are the shirts?
They are (They're) $55 each.

Do you have any in a size 42?
What is (What's) that in a European size?
Have you got any in blue?

Can I try it on?
    It fits me.   It suits me.
It does not (doesn't) fit me.

Have you got a bigger size?
This one might be better.
That one may fit better.
I will (I'll) take it.

How would you like to pay?
Can I pay by credit card?
Do you accept American Express?
Sign here, please.
Could you wrap it for me, please?

UNIT 28 Your colleagues

What does your boss look like?
Which is he?

He is (He's) the tall one with glasses.
He has (He's) got black hair.
He is (He's) wearing a grey suit.

How long has he been with the company?
He has (He's) been with the company for ten years.
Eva has been with us since last month.
She joined the department three weeks ago.
She is (She's) on the admin side.

Tom works in production.
What is (What's) he like?
He is (He's) very nice.

I think Eva has two children.
I do not (don't) think Tom is married.
    married   single
    separated   divorced

Is he divorced?
I think so.   I don't think so.

UNIT 29 Your office building

Good morning, my name is Nancy Lee.
I have an appointment with Mr Irwin.
Could you sign in, please?

If you take the lift to the second floor, they will (they'll) meet you.
This is your security pass.

I am (I'm) looking for the training department.
Is this the way to the advertising department?
Can you tell me if the boardroom is on this floor?

When you come out of the lift, turn right.
It is (It's) at the end of the corridor, on the left.
It's the last door on the right.

There is (there's) a card swipe on the left of the door.
Press the green button.

How far is it?   It's not far.
It's a long way.

You are (You're) on the wrong floor.
It is not (isn't) this way.

I do not (don't) know where it is.
I am (I'm) not sure if it's on the third floor or the fourth.

Where is (Where's) the lift?   Where are the stairs?
They are (They're) over there.

UNIT 30 How things work

How do you start the video camera?
I do not (don't) know how it works.
Do you know how to use it?

First, switch it on.
Then press the button to start it.
To start it press the green button.

Shall I show you?
You plug it in like this.
You switch it on like this.
You start it like this.

It is not (isn't) working.
I think the battery is flat.
I think the paper is jammed.

Does it usually stop like that?
Does it normally make that noise?

Where are the instructions?
What does it say?
It says, 'If it does not (doesn't) work …
… check that it is (it's) plugged in.'
… check that it's switched on.'
… call Technical Support.'

Thanks for your help.

UNIT 31 Requesting information

Could I have some information on filing cabinets?
I have your brochure here.

Could you give me the reference number, please?
    model number   catalogue number

How big is it?
It is (It's) available in three sizes – large, medium and small.

It's one metre twenty by ninety centimetres.

What colour is it?
What is it made of?
It's available in blue or red.
It comes in wood or metal.
    blue   red   green
    wood   metal   plastic

I would (I'd) like to order a large blue one.
Are they in stock?
When can you deliver?
Delivery takes three days.

Can we order online?
Go to our website. The address is offquip dot com.
Click on 'buy online'.

Thanks, I will (I'll) get back to you.

UNIT 32 Staying in a hotel

I would (I'd) like a room.
I'd like to book a room.
    to book   to reserve
    a single room   a double room
    a room with …
    … a balcony
    … a sitting room
    … a bathroom

Is it for tonight?
When is it for?
How many nights do you want the room for?

It is (It's) just for tonight.
It's for three nights.

I am (I'm) afraid we are (we're) full.
We do not (don't) have any vacancies.
What a pity!   How disappointing!

We are (We're) so busy at the moment.
It's such a busy time.
Do you have a reservation.

Would you like someone to take your bag?
No, thanks. I can carry it myself.

Can I book online?
Yes, you can make the reservation yourself.
Just go to our website and click on 'reservations'.

UNIT 33 Booking conference facilities

We are (We're) looking for a room for a conference.
How many people is it for?
Between fifty and sixty.

I think Room A is too small.
I do not (don't) think it is (it's) big enough.
Have you got anything bigger?
    bigger   smaller   cheaper

How big is Room B?
It's twenty metres long.
How wide is it?
It's fifteen metres wide.

When do you want it?
We want it on the 26th, all day.
We want it from 9 to 5.

How much do you charge?
It's €2,000 a day.
We charge €500 per hour.
That includes refreshments.

Do you provide AV equipment?
   a projector   a screen
Yes, we do.   No we don't.

Thanks, I would (I'd) like to book it.
Thanks, I will (I'll) get back to you.

UNIT 34 Organising a trip

I would (I'd) like a ticket to Bahrain.
   a single ticket   a return ticket
   business class   economy class

When do you want to travel?
Tomorrow.
On Thursday.

I will (I'll) call you …
I'll email you …
I'll text you …
   … when the tickets are ready.
   … when I have the details.
   … as soon as I arrive.

You are (You're) flying on Continental Airways.
Your flight number is CL 217.
It leaves at 09.15.
It arrives at 17.30.

How much is it going to cost?
It is (It's) £600 one way.
It's £900 return.

Is there a cheaper way?
You could go by train. That would be cheaper.
   by train   by ferry
   by bus   by plane

How do you spell Bahrain?
How do you pronounce it?

UNIT 35 Hiring a car

Where can I hire a car?
There is (There's) a place inside the airport.
There's a Hertz outside the station.
You can go online.

What size car do you want?
Have you got something like a Focus?
When do you want it?

This Monday.   Next Monday.
How long do you want it for?
A week to ten days.

We have an estate that might suit you.
What make is it?
   make   model   colour   year

The rental is $450 per week, including tax.
Does that include insurance?
The price includes unlimited mileage.

That seems OK.
That sounds very reasonable.
   seems   sounds   looks
   reasonable   cheap   expensive

Can I see your driving licence, please?
Can you fill in this form, please?
Sign here, please.

Here are the keys.

UNIT 36 Returning home

Welcome back.
It is (It's) good to have you back.
How was your trip?

It was interesting/useful/tough.
It went well.
It is good to be back.

How was Dick?
He sent you his regards.
He says 'hello'.

When did you get back?
I was booked to fly on Monday …
   … but my manager wanted me to get back early.
   … but I needed more time in Lima.
I managed to travel on Sunday instead.
I managed to reschedule.

Did you have to pay extra?
I had to upgrade to first class.
I had to pay a small supplement.
The airline was very helpful.

Did you get any firm orders?
I'm afraid not.
Is the problem delivery times?
I'm afraid so.
My report will be ready by tomorrow.

Support materials

UNIT 5 The location of your company
2 Study points

2 Work in pairs to complete the map.

Partner B's information
Your map has the information that **Partner A** requires.
You need to find out where the places below are on the map.

Glasgow   Liverpool   Birmingham   Cardiff   Southampton

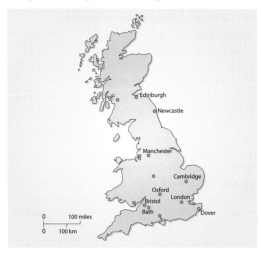

UNIT 6 The layout of your company
4 Practice

Work in pairs to understand a plan.

Partner B's information
You work for GATT. Use the information below to answer **Partner A's** questions.

e.g.   **Partner A:** What's the building opposite the main
administration block?
Partner B: It's the conference centre. The training
department is in that building.
Partner A: Where's the service centre?
Partner B: It's ...

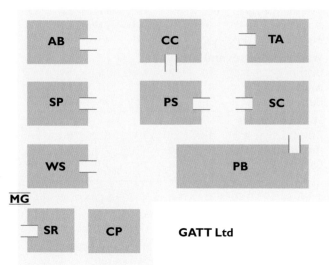

AB	Main administration block	CP	Customer car park
SC	Service centre	PS	Paint shop
TA	Testing area	SR	Showroom/Reception
WS	Warehouse and stores (Goods Inwards)	SP	Staff car park
MG	Main gate	CC	Conference centre and training department
		PB	Production building

UNIT 11 Confirming arrangements
2 Study points

1 Work in pairs to practise using embedded questions.

Partner B's information
Use the information below to help **Partner A**.

e.g. **Partner A:** Do you now when the meeting is?
   Partner B: It is on Tuesday.

	Day	Time	Place
Meeting	Tuesday	7pm	conference room
Appointment	Thursday	11.00	MD's office
Lunch	Friday	1.15	Victor's Brasserie

5 Application

Partner B's information
You are attending the meeting that **Partner A** is organising. Confirm some of the details below by phone and some by email.

Meetings	Time	Room
Tuesday's meeting	11.00	
Wednesday's meeting	10/11	317
Friday's meeting		146/247
Saturday's meeting	9.30/10.30	208

UNIT 12 Changing plans
2 Study points

4 Work in pairs to arrange a time to meet.

Partner B's information

MON	
TUES	In New York
WED	
THUR	Room booked
FRI	
SAT	

e.g. – Why don't we meet on Wednesday?
   – I'm afraid I can't.
   – What's the problem?
   – I have to ...
   – How about ...?

UNIT 13 Dealing with the unexpected
5   Application

Partner B's information
You are in your office.
Partner A's travelling to an appointment with you.

Situation 1
Partner A is an important supplier. You have a meeting with him/her in your office at 10.00. **Partner A** calls you.

Situation 2
Partner A's team is working on a project for you. They are specialist suppliers. The deadline is 12.00 tomorrow. **Partner A** calls you.

Situation 3
Partner A is a colleague. He/she is flying to your city for some meetings. Normally it is a short flight. You are meeting him/her for lunch. **Partner A** calls you.

Situation 4
Partner A works on a different site. You have a conference call booked for 2.30 with **Partner A** and a colleague in New York. **Partner A** calls you.

e.g. *Situation 1*
– I'm calling to see if we can postpone our meeting at 10.00.
– Why? What's the problem?

UNIT 15 Making contact by phone
5 Application

Work in pairs to make a telephone call.

Partner B's information
1   *Who's calling?*
    You take the call.
    • Ask who is calling.
    • Ask the caller to spell his/her name and company name.
    • Put the caller through.
2   *You're through!*
    You are the person the caller wants to speak to.
    • Answer the phone.
    • Ask the caller to repeat his/her name.

UNIT 16 Dealing with incoming calls
5   Application

Work in pairs to practise receiving calls.

Partner B's information
You receive the calls.
•   Find out who is calling.
•   Find out who she/he wants.
•   Explain why that person is not available.
•   Say when the person will be back – if you know.
•   Or transfer them to the right number.
•   Thank the caller for calling.

e.g.   **Partner A:** Can I speak to …
       Partner B: Who's calling please?

UNIT 19 Drinks and snacks
5   Application

Work in pairs to practise offering drinks and snacks.

Partner B's information
You are visiting **Partner A**.

1   You are hungry and thirsty.
2   You would like to have something else to eat and drink.
3   **Partner A** offers you light refreshments – snacks.

UNIT 21 Outings and sightseeing
5   Application

Work in pairs to practise taking a visitor on an outing.

Partner B's information
You are visiting **Partner A**.
1   Ask questions about your host's city/town/village.
2   Think about what you would like to do at the weekend. Suggest, for example, a visit to an art gallery, football match, etc. Ask about special local activities.

UNIT 26 Checking facilities and information
5   Application

Work in pairs to check what facilities are available.

Partner B's information
Partner A is working in your company for a couple of weeks. It is your job to help him/her. Look at the information below and prepare to answer his/her questions.
1   There are two free rooms. One is on the ground floor. The other one is on the first floor. There are phones in both rooms.
2   The copier and a conference phone are in your office. There's a spare laptop that has a connection to the network, which he/she can borrow.
3   You keep paper and files in a cupboard in your room.
4   There is a hole punch and a stapler on your desk.
5   He/She can ask one of the secretaries to help with his/her keying in.

UNIT 27 Shopping
4   Guided practice
Clothing sizes
(all size equivalents are approximate)

Men's suits and coats						
British	36	38	40	42	44	46	48
American	36	38	40	42	44	46	48
European	46	48	50	52	54	56	58
Men's shirts						
British	14	14½	15	15½	16	16½	17
American	14	14½	15	15½	16	16½	17
European	36	37	38	39/40	41	42	43
Men's shoes						
British	7	8	9	10	11	12	13
American	7½	8½	9½	10½	11½	12½	13½
European	40½	42	43	44½	45½	47	48
Women's dresses and suits						
British	8	10	12	14	16	18	
American	–	8	10	12	14	16	
European	–	38	40	42	44	46	
Women's shoes						
British	4	4½	5	5½	6	6½	7
American	5½	6	6½	7	7½	8	8½
European	37	37½	38	39	39½	40	40½

5   Application

Work in pairs to practise buying gifts.

Partner B's information
You are the assistant in a gift shop. Price the goods listed on page 133 and then answer **Partner A's** enquiries.

	Price
35mm films	
Earrings	
Bracelets	
Chocolate	
Sunglasses	
Phrase books	
Guide books	
Key rings	
Postcards	
Local wine	
Local souvenir (toy)	
Silk scarf	

UNIT 31 Requesting information
5 Application

1 Partner B's information

Partner A calls you for information about some items in an office furniture brochure. You take the call and deal with the enquiry, using the information below. (Items marked o/s are out of stock.)

MEETING TABLE
model no:	FC 4000X
sizes: large	(2.8m x 95cms)
medium	(1.50m x 75cms) [o/s]
small	(1.10m x 70cms)
colours:	black, brown [o/s], red
available in:	melanine, plastic, wood [o/s]

DESK
model no:	D 201-E
sizes: large	(2.85m x 1m)
standard	(1.50m x 80cms)
colours:	black [o/s], brown, white
available in:	wood [o/s], plastic, melamine (wood finish)

UNIT 33 Booking conference facilities
5 Application

Work in pairs to practise booking a hotel room for a meeting.

Partner B's information

Partner A is planning an event in a local hotel. You are the conference manager of that hotel. Answer his/her questions using the information below.

	Size	Rate	Availability	Features of all three rooms
Conference Room A	21m long 15.5m wide	€2,500 per day €2,000 per ½ day €1,000 per hour	11–21 this month 6–19 next month	•Refreshments €20 per head •Buffet lunch €30 per head •AV equipment supplied free of charge

Conference Room B	15m long 9.0m wide	€2,100 per day €1,600 per ½ day €750 per hour	1–7 this month 21–28 next month	•Refreshments €20 per head •Buffet lunch €30 per head •AV equipment supplied free of charge
Conference Room C	8.5m long 6m wide	€1,300 per day €900 per ½ day €450 per hour	7–28 this month 5–15 next month	

UNIT 35 Hiring a car
5 Application

2 Partner A: You need to question **Partner B** to fill in the form on page 119. Here is some help with the types of questions you can ask.

On the form	What you say
Name Family name/Surname First name(s)/Given name(s)	What is your name? What are your given names?
Date of birth	What is your date of birth? When were you born?
Licence no. Passport no. Issued by Issued in Issued on	What is your licence number/ passport number? Who was it issued by? Where was it issued? When was it issued?
Occupation	What is your occupation/job? What do you do?
Address Home address Work address	What is your address?
Date	What is the date (today)?
Signed	Please sign here

UNIT 36 Returning home
5 Application

Work in pairs to practise welcoming someone back from a business trip, and talking about a trip when you return.

Partner B's information
You are just back from a trip. Using the details you have agreed, talk to **Partner A** about your trip.

- Talk about the trip generally.
- Give messages or regards from people you met.
- Talk about flight changes.
- Talk about results/outcomes.

e.g. – Welcome back. How was your trip?
     – It went well. It's good to be back.

Audioscripts

UNIT 1 About you

1 Key dialogues

a – Hello, my name's Jochen Gramm. I'm from MAT in Hamburg.
  – Hi, I'm Della Lorn. I work for KLT, in Rome. Good to meet you.

b – Good morning. Are you Mr Owen from Accounts?
  – No, I'm Dick Brown from the service department. Can I help you?

c – Hello. My name's Trevor Muller. I'm in the IT department, in London.
  – Nice to meet you. I'm Sally Gigot from the Cape Town office.

d – Excuse me, are you Kate Hagel, from AB Engineering, Boston?
  – No, I'm not.
  – I'm sorry.
  – That's OK. My name's Miranda Murphy. I'm from UP Financial Services, in Dublin. I'm an accountant, not an engineer. Here's my card.

4 Listening

a My name's Ole Boysen. I'm from Stockholm in Sweden, but I work in Brussels. I work for PLP International – it's a multinational company. We're in computer software. I'm in the finance department. I'm an accountant. I'd like to come to your conference. My number is 073 6125 144.

b Hello, this is Sonya Gonin. I'm a sales rep – I work for AC Computers. It's a Korean company, but I work in the Australian office, in Sydney. I'm in the sales department. The number is 070 36 4188 95. Could you call me back, please?

UNIT 2 About your job

1 Key dialogues

a – What do you do?
  – I work for a bank in Vancouver.
  – Which one?
  – Credit West. I'm in the IT department.

b – You work for a law firm …
  – Yes I do,
  – Are you a lawyer?
  – No, I'm on the finance side. I'm the deputy finance director.

c – Are you on the sales side?
  – No I work in Maintenance.
  – What do you do?
  – I'm an electrical engineer.

d – What's your job?
  – I work for a toy manufacturer called Games Inc. I'm in the European sales team.
  – Do you like it?
  – Yes, it's OK. I'm the assistant manager.

2 Study points

3 a Erawan Manufacturing – that's E-R-A-W-A-N.
  b Nakanoshima Engineering – that's N-A-K-A-N-O-S-H-I-M-A.
  c Kiruna – you spell that K-I-R-U-N-A, Kiruna Oil.
  d Z-A-G-O-R-S-K, Zagorsk Trading.
  e Dobbie Associates – that's D-O-double B-I-E.
  f Loftleider Industries – Loftleider is spelt L-O-F-T-L-E-I-D-E-R.
  g B-A-C-O-L-O-D, Bacolod Services.
  h Skreen-Kwik Advertising – that's S-K-R-E-E-N hyphen K-W-I-K.

UNIT 3 About where you work

1 Key dialogues

a – He works in the centre of town.
  – Where?
  – In Delta Square. His office is on the first floor. They have a car park in the basement.

b – Where do you work?
  – In a business park near the airport.
  – Do you have a canteen?
  – No.
  – Where do you have lunch?
  – In the airport. There are some good cafes there.

c – Where does she work?
  – In a factory in Moscow Road.
  – Where's that?
  – Near the station. Her department is on the third floor.

d – We must meet for lunch.
  – Yes, where do you work?
  – I work in a warehouse not far from the centre.
  – Oh, are there any good restaurants or cafes nearby?
  – No, but we have an excellent canteen.

4 Listening

Dialogue 1
 – Where do you work?
 – In Lisbon Road, number fifteen. It's a big building. My office is on the first floor.
 – What is it? What do you do?
 – It's a warehouse. I'm a stock control manager.
 – And where's Lisbon Road?
 – It's near the station.
 – Oh, I know. There are some good cafes round there. We must meet for coffee.
 – That's an excellent idea.
 – Are you free tomorrow?
 – What time?
 – Eleven?
 – Eleven is fine.

Dialogue 2
 – I work in the centre of town.
 – Whereabouts?
 – In Moscow Road.

- There are some good bars round there. We must meet for a drink.
- Or we could meet for lunch. There are some excellent restaurants nearby.
- OK, what's your address?
- It's number thirty-seven.
- Is that near the post office?
- No, the post office is in Moscow Drive.
- Oh, yes.
- We're in Moscow Road. It's a big office building. I'm on the sixth floor.
- Do you have a car park?
- Yes, there's car parking in the basement.

UNIT 4 Your business activities
1 Key dialogues

a – We make parts for the car industry. We do ninety per cent of our business in France. We don't export much. We're a small company.
– What are you working on at the moment?
– I'm developing a new management information system. I'm a computer programmer.

b – What does your company do?
– We sell shoes and leather goods.
– How's business?
– It isn't very good. We aren't making much money at the moment. Things are quiet.

c – I'm in the insurance business.
– Who do you work for?
– Amtak – our head office is in Frankfurt, but do a lot of business in the Far East. We're building a new office in Thailand at the moment.
– Do you do much business in Australia?
– No, not much.

d – We're in IT. We're developing new anti-virus software at the moment.
– Is business going well?
– Yes, in some markets – we're doing a lot of business in Western Europe.

3 Listening

Tektron Computers
– We make computers. One of our main markets is South America. We also do a lot of business in Central America. About thirteen per cent of our sales is in that area.
– Do you do any business in Africa?
– Not much – our products sell in North Africa, but it's a small market.

Universal Trading
– We manufacture and sell shoes. We're building a factory in Russia at the moment. We do about twenty-five per cent of our business in Eastern Europe.
– Do you do much business in Western Europe?
– It's not our main market, but we sell quite a lot there.
– Do you export to South-East Asia?
– Yes, but not very much.

Nexpol Insurance
– We're in the insurance business.
– Where is your main market?

– Western Europe.
– What about the Middle East?
– We have an office in Cairo, but it isn't a big market. We do about nine or ten per cent of our business in that area. Europe is over fifty per cent.
– Do you do business in South America?
– Yes, but it's a new market for us. We're developing new products for the area. But we aren't selling much at the moment.

UNIT 5 The location of your company
1 Key dialogues

a – Where are your main offices in Japan?
– We have two.
– Where are they?
– One is in the centre of Osaka, the other is twenty kilometres to the south, near a place called Izumi.

b – Do you have an agent in Malaysia?
– Yes, his office is south of Kuala Lumpur, in a place called Malacca.
– Is it far from Singapore?
– It's about one hundred and seventy kilometres away.

c – What about Vietnam?
– We have a representative in the south of the country, but not in the north. He's in Cholon.
– Where is that exactly?
– It's about thirty kilometres south-west of Ho Chi Minh City.

d – What about Korea?
– Yes, we have two factories in Korea. One is forty kilometres west of Seoul in Inchon. The other one is in the south of the country, in Pusan.

4 Application

THB is a small engineering company. They make parts for the car industry. They have two factories in the west of the country, and distributors in the north, south and east. Two hundred and twenty people work for the company; one hundred and fifty men, and seventy women.

UNIT 6 The layout of your company
1 Key dialogues

a – That's the main production building.
– And where's the service department?
– It's behind that warehouse over there.
– Is it this way?
– No, you go down that road over there.

b – Is the accounts department in this building?
– Yes, it's on the third floor. The entrance is opposite the lift.
– I have an appointment with Zeenat Hussein.
– I'll call her. What's your name?
– Paul Triani.
– Can you sign in, please?
– (On phone) Hello – reception here. We have Mr Triani. OK, thanks.
(To Triani) Take the lift to the third floor and she'll meet you at the lift. This is your visitor's pass.

c – What's this place?
– It's the IT department.

- Where's the help desk?
- Help desk and user support are through those doors on the right.

d – Excuse me, where's the toilet?
- It's downstairs in the basement. Go down these stairs and turn left – it's the second door on the left.

3 Listening

Dialogue 1
- Good morning
- Hello, I'm Libby Fanon of Bax Tools. I have an appointment with Mr Adam in Production.
- Can you sign in, please?
- Yes.
- Where are you from?
- Bax Tools.
- Is that B-A-X?
- Yes.
- Yes, he's expecting you. Production is in that building over there. This is your visitor's pass.
- Thanks.

Dialogue 2
- Good morning. I'm visiting the accounts department.
- What's your name, please?
- Sunita Das.
- And your company?
- Asia Trading.
- Asia Trading. And who are you visiting?
- The Manager, Mr Malick.
- (On phone) Hello, this is reception. We have a visitor for Mr Malick, Miss Sunita Das …
- Mrs …
- Oh sorry, it's Mrs Das. OK. (To Das) Right, you need this visitor's pass. The accounts department is that way, in the first building past the car park. It's on the third floor.

UNIT 7 Meeting and welcoming
1 Key dialogues

a – Good afternoon. My name's Gerry Scalia. I'd like to welcome you to TZ. This is Clare Hanan, our PR Manager.
- Hello, it's nice to meet you all. How was your trip?
- It was OK.

b – Hi, it's good to see you. How was your flight?
- Not good. The plane was two hours late.
- Oh, dear. Was the hotel OK?
- Yes, it was fine.

c – Good morning. Welcome back. How was your trip to Britain?
- It was awful.
- Oh, dear. Why?
- The trains were late and the weather was terrible.
- Were the hotel arrangements OK?
- No, they weren't.

d – This is Mrs Walchia.
- How do you do?
- Pleased to meet you.
- How was your journey?

- Er …
- Mrs Walchia is from Romania.
- I'm sorry, I don't speak Romanian.
- That's OK, I speak English. Well, I speak a little English. My journey was good.

3 Listening

First meeting
- Hi. I'm Ivan Kovacic.
- Hello. My name's Gracie Mayers.
- Nice to meet you.
- It's nice to meet you, too.
- Do you work here?
- No.

Second meeting
- Good morning, John.
- Good morning, Victor.
- How are you today?
- Not too bad. How are you?
- Oh fine.

Third meeting
- Hello, how was your trip?
- It was terrible. My contact was ill.
- Oh no!
- And the plane was two hours late.
- Oh dear! Anyway, welcome back.

Fourth meeting
- This is Pat Ollis from the Rio office.
- Hi, my name's Luis Pinto.
- Pleased to meet you, Luis. Where are you from?
- I work for KRT in Mexico City.
- How was your flight?
- Fine.

UNIT 8 The first two minutes
1 Key dialogues

a – Hello, Freya. How's life?
- Fine, How about you?
- Oh, not too bad. And how are your family?
- They're all fine too.
- That's good.

b – When are you leaving?
- Friday morning.
- Are you doing anything tomorrow evening?
- No I'm not.

c – So how do you like New York?
- I really like it.
- Is this your first visit to the States?
- Yes, it is.
- How long are you here for?
- Three days.
- Have a good stay.

d – How are you?
- Very well.
- How's business?
- It's going very well.
- I hear you're leaving tomorrow.
- That's right. I'm flying home tomorrow morning.
- What are you doing this evening?

4 Listening

Dialogue 1

– How's your family?
– Very well. How are you?
– Not too bad. How long are you here for?
– I'm leaving tomorrow morning.
– We must meet for a drink. What are you doing this evening?
– I'm meeting our distributor.
– OK, see you next time you are here. Enjoy your stay.
– Thanks.
– Send me an email next time you're coming.

Dialogue 2

– How long are you here for?
– I'm leaving on Thursday.
– Is this your first visit to Sydney?
– No, we have a sales office here.
– What do you do?
– I'm in IT support. We're an on-line wedding list company. So the IT side is important.
– How do you like Sydney?
– I really like it.
– Well, have a good stay.
– Thanks.

UNIT 9 Partings and thanks

1 Key dialogues

a – Thanks for the lunch.
  – You're welcome.
  – And I'll see you next week.
  – Yes, see you. Bye.
  – Bye.

b – Have a good flight.
  – Thanks, and thanks for everything.
  – Well, thank you for coming.
  – Don't forget to keep in touch.
  – I won't. And I'll see you in the New Year.
  – Bye.

c – Give my regards to your MD.
  – I will. I'll call you next week.
  – OK. By then. See you soon.
  – See you. Bye.

d – Thanks for your help.
  – It's my pleasure. You must visit us again soon.
  – I will.
  – Don't forget to send those figures.
  – I'll email them tomorrow.
  – Keep in touch.

4 Listening

a – Many thanks for all your help.
  – Not at all. It's my pleasure.
  – And I'll see you next week.
  – Yes, see you then. Bye.
  – Bye.

b – Have a good journey home.
  – Thank you, and thanks for everything.
  – No problem. You're welcome.
  – Don't forget to keep in touch.

  – I won't. Bye.
  – Goodbye.

c – Give my regards to everyone in the sales office.
  – I will.
  – And don't forget to ring me next week.
  – I won't. Thanks for your help.

d – You must come and see us again soon.
  – Thank you, but first you must visit us.
  – That would be great. So, have a good flight home.
  – Thanks for all your hospitality.
  – No problem. See you soon.

UNIT 10 Setting up a meeting

1 Key dialogues

a – Can we meet for lunch on the 13th?
  – No, I'll be in London then.
  – How about the 12th?
  – Yes, that's fine.
  – Fine, I'll see you then.

b – Is Tuesday OK?
  – No, I'm afraid I can't make Tuesday.
  – What about Wednesday?
  – Yes, that's fine.

c – Can you come to a meeting tomorrow morning?
  – No, I'm sorry, I can't. But I'm free in the afternoon.
  – OK, let's meet in the afternoon.
  – What time?
  – Can you make 1.30?
  – Sorry, I'm not free till two.
  – OK, let's meet at 2.30.

d – What's the date?
  – It's the 17th.
  – Can you make the meeting on the 20th?
  – What day is that?
  – It's Wednesday.
  – Yes, that's fine.
  – Good. See you then.

4 Listening

– Thanks for your email about the review meeting.
– Can you make it?
– That's why I'm calling. I'm afraid I'm in Philadelphia on Wednesday. What date is that?
– The 19th.
– Yeah, I am. What time's the meeting?
– It's in the morning – 10.30.
– There's no way I can make it. I have meetings with customers in our Philadelphia office till 2.30.
– Are you back in the office on Thursday?
– Yes, I am.
– OK, let's meet on Thursday morning.
– What time?
– Can you make nine o'clock?
– Yes, that's fine.
– Oh – the meeting room isn't free then.
– We can meet in your office.
– Right.

UNIT 11 Confirming arrangements

1 Key dialogues

a – I'm calling about tomorrow's meeting. Is it at ten
   or eleven?
   – It's at eleven.
   – And can I check the place?
   – It's in Petra's office.
   – Thanks.

b – Are you still OK for Monday?
   – Yes, I am.
   – The meeting is at 4.30, not five. Is that OK?
   – I'm not sure.
   – Could you let me know?
   – Of course.

c – Is Monday's meeting still OK?
   – Yes, it is.
   – Do you know when it is yet?
   – Yes, it's at 9.15.
   – And do you know where it is?
   – Room 703.

d – I'm calling to confirm our meeting.
   – Which meeting?
   – The one on Wednesday.
   – Oh, yes. Sorry, it's not in my diary.
   – Can you still make it?
   – Yes, it's fine. Thanks for reminding me.

3 Listening

– I'm calling to confirm the arrangements for
  Mr Amosu's visit.
– Oh, yes, hold on. I'll get the schedule up on the screen.
  Right, go ahead.
– The meeting with Victoria is at 9.30, is that right?
– Yes, it is.
– Do you know where it is yet?
– Yes, it's in Mr Trigg's office.
– Trigg's office … OK. Now, can I check the meeting with the
  management committee? Is it still in the boardroom?
– Yes, it is.
– Do you have a time yet?
– Yes, it's at 10.30.
– Right. Now, is Peter Sallis still OK for the meeting at
  eleven? I believe he's in Russia.
– He's coming back on Tuesday.
– Good. Do you know where the meeting is yet?
– No, I'm afraid we don't.
– Can you let me know, please?
– Yes, of course.
– OK, that's good. Could you confirm those details?
– Yes, of course.
– Thanks for your help.
– Thank you for calling.

UNIT 12 Changing plans

1 Key dialogues

a – Can we change the time of next week's meeting?
   – Why? What's the problem?
   – The conference room is booked in the morning.
   – It'll be free after lunch.
   – I can't make it then because I have to meet a client.

b – We'll have to change the room. The boardroom's
   occupied.
   – Why don't we start later?
   – OK, let's start at ten.
   – Will it be free by then?
   – I'll find out.

c – I'm afraid all the meeting rooms are reserved.
   – We'll have to begin earlier.
   – We can't do that.
   – Why not?
   – The people from LTK can't come before eleven.
   – Why don't we meet in your office?
   – OK, let's do that.

d – John can't make Monday's meeting.
   – Why not?
   – He won't be back from Brussels till after lunch.
   – Will he be back by four?
   – Yes, he will.
   – OK, let's change it to 4.15.

2 Study points

The conference room is booked.
i A Swiss managing director: 'How about meeting in Room
  number 12?'
ii A Sierra Leonean administrative assistant: 'Could we try
  Room 8 instead?'
iii An Egyptian importer: 'Is there another room we can use?'
iv A Canadian HR manager: 'Why don't we meet after lunch?'
v A Welsh IT manager: 'Let's try and book another room.'

5 Application

– I'm afraid we'll have to change the time of next week's
  management meeting.
– Why? What's the problem?
– Well, the Sales Manager is away that day, and the
  conference room is booked.
– Oh no …
– When will she be back?
– She's coming back on the 15th.
– Is the conference room free on the 15th?
– It's free from 12.30.
– Will she be back by then?
– Yes, she will.
– OK, let's meet at 12.30.

UNIT 13 Dealing with the unexpected

1 Key dialogues

a – Three members of the team are down with a virus, and
   the work isn't going to be ready. I'm sorry.
   – I'm sorry about your team. How are they?
   – Not good …
   – When do you think you can deliver?
   – Could we postpone the deadline till next Wednesday?
   – OK, but keep me informed.

b – About the conference call.
   – Yes, is everything OK?
   – No, I'm afraid not. I'm calling to ask if we could put
   it off?
   – Why? What's the problem?
   – Our system is down and we can't access the files. I'm

sorry about this.
– Don't worry – these things happen.

c – Look, I'm sorry but I'm not going to make the meeting? There's a security alert and the airport is closed.
– Sorry to hear that. Are you OK?
– Yes, I'm fine. I'll call you when I get back to the office.

d – I'm calling about our lunch date. Could we call it off? There's been a crash and the motorway is completely blocked. I'm not going to make it. I'm sorry.
– That's OK. I can't make it either. My plane is delayed.

3 Listening

a – I'm calling about tomorrow's deadline.
– Is there a problem?
– Yes, I'm afraid there is. The work isn't going to be ready.
– We'll have to cancel the meeting. What's the problem?
– We're having IT problems. We can't access the files.
– So when is the work going to be ready.
– It's going to take another two days – if we can get into the system.
– OK – keep me informed.

b – Could we postpone our conference call with Detroit?
– When is it?
– At 10.30.
– OK – what's the problem?
– There's a security alert and our office is closed.
– What! Are you OK?
– Yes, I'm fine but my laptop and files are in the office. Could we put it off till this afternoon? I'm sorry about this.
– Sure – don't worry.

c – Look, I'm sorry but I can't make our lunch date.
– What's wrong?
– I'm stuck in traffic. There's been a crash and the motorway is blocked. I'm sorry.
– That's OK – don't worry. There are problems here too. My assistant is ill and we have a big project to finish.
– When's the deadline.
– Three o'clock.
– Let's meet next week.
– OK – thanks for letting me know.

UNIT 14 Explaining and apologising
1 Key dialogues

a – I'm sorry I'm late.
– What happened? Did you have a problem with the train?
– No, our meeting overran. I'm very sorry.
– That's OK. Don't worry.

b – I'm sorry I missed our appointment.
– That's OK. It's not a problem.
– I had to meet a customer. I wanted to call you but I didn't have your details with me.

c – I apologise for forgetting the meeting.
– What happened?
– I had to take my children to school because my wife isn't well. I'm afraid I forgot about the meeting.
– Oh, don't worry. Is your wife OK?
– Yes, she just has flu. It's nothing serious.
– That's good …

d – I'm really sorry I missed our lunch date.
– Did you lose the address?
– No, I didn't. I had to finish some work. We're very busy at the moment. I tried to call you, but I didn't have your number in my address book.
– That's OK. It's not a problem.

4 Application

a – How was the conference?
– I didn't go.
– Oh, why not?
– I was very busy. I didn't have time.
– Did you phone them?
– No, I didn't. I wanted to call, but I'm afraid I forgot.

b – Did you miss the appointment?
– Yes, I did.
– What happened?
– My husband wasn't well and I had to take him to hospital.
– Oh, I'm sorry. Is he OK?
– Yes, it wasn't serious. But I was worried and I forgot about the appointment. I'm sorry.
– That's OK. Don't worry.

c – Did you go to the meeting?
– No, I'm afraid I didn't.
– What happened?
– Well, I had lunch with a client, and I'm afraid I missed the train.

UNIT 15 Making contact by phone
1 Key dialogues

a – Hello, can I speak to Mr Semler, please?
– Speaking.
– Hello, this is Manuel Postigo from DRK. I'm calling about the conference next week. Is it possible to send me some more information?
– Yes, of course. Could you give me your address, please?
– It's postigo h@drk.com
– Could you repeat that please?

b – Hello.
– Hello, is that Mr Druper?
– Speaking.
– Oh, hello. Richard Peace here. Could you tell me something about the conference?
– Yes, of course, Richard. What would you like to know?

c – Is that Pete?
– No, this is Hans.
– Hello, Hans. It's Lydia Booker here.
– Hi.
– I'm calling about the conference.

d – Can I speak to Pete Karob, please?
– Who's calling?
– Rosa Kleeb.
– Is that K-L-E-E-B?
– Yes, that's right.
– I'm sorry, his extension is on voicemail. Would you like to leave a message?
– No, I'll try again later.
– Thank you for calling.

4 Listening

a – Blair Associates. Good morning.
 – Can I speak to Anna Blair, please?
 – Can I have your name, please?
 – Yes, it's Beth Hogan.
 – And your company?
 – CATT Ltd. That's spelt C-A-double T. It's about the meeting on Friday.
 – Thank you, Miss Hogan. I'll try her extension.

b – Blair Associates. Good morning.
 – Can you put me through to Anna Blair, please?
 – Who's calling?
 – It's Roland Lancy from Brel, that's B-R-E-L. I'm calling about Anna's visit to Paris next week.
 – Thank you, Mr Lancy. One moment, please. Putting you through …

c – Hello. Is it possible to speak to Anna Blair?
 – Who's calling, please?
 – My name's Barbara Lederman.
 – And you're calling from?
 – IKAL, that's I-K-A-L. I'm calling about the seminar in Amsterdam.
 – Just a moment, please. I'll put you through. I'm sorry her extension is on voicemail. Would you like to leave a message.
 – No, I'll try her again later.

UNIT 16 Dealing with incoming calls
1 Key dialogues

a – Hello, is that Mr Waltanen?
 – You're through to the wrong extension. Who do you want?
 – Mr Waltanen.
 – You need extension 417. Hold on – I'll transfer you.

b – Hello, Janet.
 – Oh, hello, Fabio. I'm afraid I can't talk now. I'm in a meeting. Can I call you back?
 – Of course. I'll be in the office until quarter past four.
 – Fine. I'll call you later.

c – Hello, Roger. Is Magda back from holiday?
 – No, I'm afraid she's away for two more days. Can she call you when she gets back?
 – Thanks. I'll be here until the end of the week.

d – Mrs Rill's number is on voicemail. Would you like to leave a message or would you like to speak to someone else?
 – Does she have an assistant?
 – Hold on – I'll find out.

4 Listening

Call 1
 – I'm afraid he's away from his desk at the moment. Can I get him to call you?
 – Do you know when he will be back?
 – He's probably at lunch.
 – Thanks – I'll call later.

Call 2
I'm either away from my desk or on the phone. Leave a message and I'll get back to you when I'm free.

Call 3
I'm out of the office till the 27th. If your query is urgent, please contact Dora Flegg on extension 471.

Call 4
 – Her extension is on voicemail.
 – Is she still on holiday?
 – No, her calls are forwarded to me because she's in a meeting.

Call 5
 – Can I speak to Tebor?
 – You're through to the wrong extension. Hold on, I'll transfer you.

UNIT 17 Leaving and taking messages
1 Key dialogues

a – Could you give Ali a message, please?
 – Yes, of course.
 – Could you ask him to call Fernando Robles – that's R-O-B-L-E-S – on 223 987? I'll be at that number until five o'clock.
 – Sure, I'll give him the message.
 – Thanks. Bye.

b – Can I leave a message for Bruno?
 – Yes, of course. Go ahead.
 – Please tell him that Jan Nagel from Atco called, and that I'll call again tomorrow morning.
 – I'll tell him.
 – Thanks. Bye.

c – Hi. Is Hamid Kumal there?
 – No, I'm afraid he's not at his desk. Can I take a message?
 – Thanks. Could you say that Elena Roche called. Could you ask him to call me back before six?

d – I'm afraid Mr Kumal isn't here at the moment. Can I take a message?
 – Yes, I wanted to check he received my messages. I sent him an email and I left a voicemail on his mobile.
 – Sorry, I didn't catch your name.
 – It's Svensson. S-V-E-N-S-S-O-N.
 – Thank you Mr Svensson. I'll tell him.

4 Listening

a – Is Andrew there?
 – No, I'm afraid he's at lunch. Can I help you?
 – Yes, thanks. Could you give him a message for me?
 – Yes, of course.
 – Could you tell him that Magda called? Could you ask him to call me back before five? My number is 7292. Did you get that?
 – No, sorry, could you say it again?
 – Yes, of course, 7292.
 – Fine. I'll give him the message.
 – Many thanks.

b – Hello.
  – Andrew?
  – No, it's Dick Rowntree speaking. Can I help you?
  – Yes, thanks. Could you ask Andrew to call Philippe Buzet before Friday?
  – Sorry, could you spell your name, please?
  – Yes, it's Philippe Buzet. That's Buzet spelt B-U-Z-E-T.
  – Thanks, and has he got your number?
  – Yes, but I'll give it to you just in case. It's 90876.
  – Fine. I'll tell him to call you.

UNIT 18 Email and telephone problems
1 Key dialogues

a – Pat Sookia.
  – Hello, Miss Sookia. Peter Wong here. I'm sorry I didn't make contact this morning. I tried at about nine, but I couldn't get through.
  – Was there a problem with the phone?
  – No, I had the wrong number. I had your old number in my mobile.

b – Igor, where are you?
  – I'm in my car. I'm forwarding my calls to my mobile.
  – Igor … you're breaking up. Can you repeat that?
  – Can you hear me now?
  – Yes, I can now.
  – My battery is low. Give me your number and I'll call you on a land line.

c – I'm trying to send you an email but it keeps bouncing back. Can I check your address?
  – Yes, it's john d, one word, at e l d dot com.
  – Oh, I've got 'john dot d' – I'll try again …

d – I called just after lunch but your number was on voicemail.
  – Yes, I had a conference call.
  – Did you get my message?
  – I'll just check. Can I put you on hold?
  – Yes, of course.

4 Listening

Dialogue 1
  – I sent you the information in an email.
  – I don't think I got it. It's not in my inbox. Could you resend it? We're having some problems with our system.

Dialogue 2
  – I'm trying to get through to Bella Senik. I'm going straight through to her voicemail.
  – She is forwarding her calls to her mobile. She's probably in a meeting.

Dialogue 3
  – I couldn't open the attachment. Could you send it in another format?
  – I'll try to send it in Word. Call me if you still can't open it.

Dialogue 4
  – I can't log on?
  – Are you using your new user name and password?
  – Did they change?
  – Didn't you get my email?

Dialogue 5
  – Is that Martine Guyon?
  – No it's Sandy Harris. You've come through to the wrong extension.
  – What's Martine's extension number? Do you know?
  – No, I'm sorry, I don't. Hold on – I'll find out for you.

Dialogue 6
  – Can you hear me now? It's a bad line.
  – That's better.
  – I'll see you on Friday.
  – Sorry? You're breaking up again. Can you repeat that?
  – I'll call you back when I get to the office.
  – OK.

UNIT 19 Drinks and snacks
1 Key dialogues

a – Shall we take a short break?
  – That's a good idea.
  – Would you like a cup of coffee?
  – Yes, please.
  – How do you like it?
  – Black, no sugar, please.

b – Can I get you anything else?
  – Yes, can I have a biscuit?
  – Yes, of course. You must be hungry. Try these chocolate ones. They're very good.
  – Thanks.
  – Another one?
  – No, thanks.

c – Is this your coffee, John?
  – No, I think that one's mine, the one without milk.
  – Do you take sugar?
  – No, thanks.

d – Can I get you a sandwich?
  – No, thanks.
  – Would you like one of these cakes?
  – Yes, please. Thanks. Mmmm, they're delicious.

3 Listening

  – Would you like something? Coffee? Tea? Juice? A soft drink? And what about something to eat? There are some rolls and sandwiches. What would you like?
  – A cup of coffee, please. What sandwiches do you have?
  – Cheese, salad or beef.
  – Can I have cheese?
  – Of course. I'll have a cheese one too. This one's for you.
  – Thanks.
  – Do you take sugar?
  – No thanks.
  – Can I pass you the milk?
  – Thanks.
  – Can I get you anything else? A biscuit or something?

UNIT 20 Eating out
1 Key dialogues

a A: Would you like to go out for a meal tomorrow night?
  B: That's a good idea.
  A: Do you like Mexican food?

B: Yes, I do.
A: Good. I know a very good Mexican restaurant. We could go there.

b A: Excuse me. But can we have the menu, please?
W: The beef is very good, and I recommend the chicken.
A: I'll have the beef.
B: Chicken for me, please.

c A: Excuse me, the food is cold.
W: Oh, I'm very sorry. I'll change it for you.

d W: Would you like a dessert?
A: Yes, a small piece of cake, please.
B: Just a cup of coffee for me, please.
W: Would you like your coffee now?
B: No thanks, I'll have it later.
W: And would you like coffee?
A: No, thank you.

e A: Can I have the bill, please? Thank you. Does it include service?
W: No, it doesn't. The 17½ per cent is VAT.
A: Thank you very much. We enjoyed the meal.
W: Thank you.

3 Listening

– Are you ready to order?
– Yes, I'd like a fillet steak, please, with vegetables and french fried potatoes.
– How would you like your steak?
– Medium, please.
– Thank you. And would you like a starter?
– Yes, I think I'll have the mushroom soup.
– And for dessert?
– Cheese and biscuits. And can I have half a bottle of your house red wine?
– Yes, of course. Thank you very much.

UNIT 21 Outings and sightseeing
1 Key dialogues

a – Have you been to Valencia before?
– No, this is my first visit here, but I've spent some time in Barcelona.
– Oh, when were you last in Barcelona?
– It was about two years ago.
– Have you been to the Gaudi Cathedral?
– Yes, I have.

b – Would you like to go for a drive round?
– Yes, I'd enjoy that.
– We could drive into the centre of town. There's a festival on.
– What kind of festival is it?
– I think it's a beer festival.

c – That building is the oldest in the town.
– How old is it?
– I'm not sure. Over 300 years, I think.
– It's very beautiful.
– I agree.

d – I have a spare ticket for *Tosca* this evening. Would you like to come?
– Yes, please. I love opera, but I've never seen *Tosca*.

– Fine. Where are you staying?
– At the Ritz.
– Right, I'll pick you up at 6.30.

3 Listening

– Do you have any plans for the weekend?
– No, nothing special.
– Fine. Would you like to go to the ballet on Saturday night? I've got some tickets for *Swan Lake* at the Coliseum.
– Yes, I'd love to. I've never been to a ballet, or an opera.
– Well, I'm sure you'll enjoy it. And what about doing something on Saturday afternoon?
– Fine, what do you suggest?
– Have you ever been to a cricket match?
– No, but I've seen it on satellite TV.
– Well, cricket's a possibility. What about football or rugby? There are some good matches on Saturday.
– I've seen a lot of football, but I've never been to a rugby match. That would be interesting.
– That suits me. We could go and see the Saracens. They're our local team.

UNIT 22 Starting a journey
1 Key dialogues

a – Excuse me, can I check-in for Manila here?
– Yes, sir. Can I see your ticket and passport, please? Thank you. Would you like an aisle seat or a window seat?
– An aisle seat, please – if possible.

b – Do I have to clear customs in Helsinki?
– No, it's a through flight. There are customs facilities in Tampere. Do you have any hand luggage?
– Yes, one piece.
– Did you pack your bag yourself?
– Yes, I did.

c – Excuse me, I think that's my seat.
– Oh, I'm sorry. I'll move.
– Can I put your bag up for you?
– Yes, please. Thanks.
– Do you need your coat?
– Yes, please.

d – Can I have a single to Avignon?
– Yes, that's thirty-two euros.
– When does it leave?
– The train leaves at 14.15.
– And which platform is it?
– Go to platform 9.

3 Listening

e.g.– This is the final call for Finnair flight AY345 to Helsinki. Will all passengers please proceed to Gate 14.
a – The next Eurostar train from Waterloo to Gare du Nord will depart from platform 1 at 19.03.
b – Will Mr Chang travelling on British Airways flight BA987 to Bangkok please proceed to Gate 17 immediately.
c – Would all passengers for the direct train to Chicago Union Station please go to platform 9, where the delayed 17.19 service will now depart at 17.43.

d – Will the last remaining passengers please proceed to Gate 6 where Japan Airlines Flight JL392 is now closing.

5 Application

– Excuse me, is this the right check-in for Dallas?
– Yes, it is. Can I see your ticket and passport please? … and how many bags do you have to check in?
– None, I just have hand luggage. Can I have an aisle seat?
– Yes, we have one left.
– Good, I have long legs so I need some space! I'm flying on to Los Angeles – it's a long flight. Do I need to clear customs in Dallas?
– No, you can clear customs in Los Angeles.
– Fine.
– Here's your boarding card. It's Gate 16, boarding at 4.10. Have a good flight.
– Thank you.

UNIT 23 Travelling
1 Key dialogues

a – Do you know when we get into Sydney?
– We're due in at five o'clock, but I think we're going to be late.

b – Excuse me, have you got today's English newspapers?
– No, I'm afraid I haven't. I'll try and find one for you later.
– Thanks.

c – Sorry.
– That's all right. Have you got enough room?
– Yes, I have thanks.

d – Excuse me, are we on time?
– Yes, we expect to land in twenty minutes.

e – Excuse me, I don't know this area. Can you tell me when we arrive at the bus stop for Madison Avenue?
– Sit near the front of the bus and I'll call you when it's your stop.

f – Is there a bus service into town?
– Yes, the stop is just outside the terminal building.
– Do you know how much it costs?
– I think it's twenty dollars.

3 Listening

– Excuse me, what time do we arrive in Frankfurt?
– We're due in at 10.15, but unfortunately we're going to be half an hour late. Would you like a drink from the bar?
– Yes, please. Can I have a mineral water? Thank you. How much is that?
– Nothing, sir. The drinks are complimentary.
– Thank you. Could you tell me if there's a bus from the airport to the city centre?
– There is. The stop is just outside the main terminal building. There's also a train.
– Thanks. Do you know how much the fare is?
– No, I'm sorry I don't know. It isn't expensive.

UNIT 24 Arriving and meeting contacts
A1 Key dialogues

a – Hello, Ivana. It's good to see you again.
– How was the journey?
– Very good, thanks. No problems.
– Shall I take your bag? My car's in the car park, just over there.

b – How was the weather in Scotland?
– Awful. It was raining when I left. It was worse than it is here.
– What was the temperature like?
– Five degrees. It was freezing.

c – Hello, Marco. We were getting worried about you.
– Yes, I'm sorry I'm late. The plane was delayed.
– Why was that?
– There was a lot of snow on the runway.

d – So, shall we run through your programme?
– Yes, of course.
– We had to make some changes.
– Why was that?
– The people in Edinburgh couldn't meet us on Tuesday.

3 Listening

JR: Hello. You must be Carita Drago from ROS.
CD: Yes, that's right.
JR: Nice to meet you. My name's Janet Riga. I've come to take you to the hotel.
CD: Thank you very much. It's very kind of you to meet me.
JR: It's my pleasure. Can I help you with your luggage? My car's in the car park, just over there.
CD: Thanks. I think I can manage.
JR: We had to make some changes to your schedule next week. I'll tell you about them in the car … Shall I put these in the car for you?
CD: Thank you. That's very kind of you.

UNIT 25 Gifts and saying thank you
1 Key dialogues

a – Well, thank you. I really enjoyed that.
– So did I. I thought the orchestra was excellent.
– Can I give you a lift back to the hotel?
– No, thanks. It's not far. I think I'll walk back.

b – Many thanks for showing me round.
– It's my pleasure.
– I really enjoyed looking round the harbour.
– So did I, but I didn't like the weather much.
– Neither did I. It was terrible.

c – Thank you for organising everything so well.
– Not at all. My secretary did everything.
– Well, please pass on my thanks. Everything went very well.
– It did.
– I saw everyone I wanted to see.

d – This is for you.
– That's very kind of you. Can I open it?
– Yes, of course.
– It's beautiful. Thank you very much indeed.

- I'm glad you like it.
- I love it.

3 Listening

- Well, it's been an extremely useful trip. Thank you for organising everything and for looking after us so well. We've done everything we planned to do.
- Well, thank you for coming. We've really enjoyed having you, and we hope you'll come and see us again next year.
- Thank you. We'd love to come back next year. And now can I give you this as a small 'thank you' present? It's a painting by one of our local artists. I hope you like it.
- Oh, it's beautiful. Thank you very much indeed.

UNIT 26 Checking facilities
1 Key dialogues

a
- Can I use your phone?
- Yes, of course. You need to dial zero to get an outside line.
- Thanks. Where can I scan this document?
- You can use the scanner in my office.

b
- Excuse me, I need some things for the presentation this afternoon.
- Sure, what do you need?
- A flipchart, a projector and an extension lead.
- The extension lead is in this cupboard. I think there's a spare flipchart in the boardroom. And I'll check when the projector will be available.

c
- Could you print the handouts for tomorrow's meeting? I have them on disk.
- When do you need them?
- Could I have them by ten? The meeting is at eleven.
- That's no problem. Leave them with me. I'll do it this afternoon.

d
- Vishalee, there's something wrong with my computer. It won't shut down. Do you know who I can ask to fix it?
- Why don't you call the Help Desk? I'm sure they'll help you.

3 Listening

- How's business at the moment?
- Fine, but we think we need a new image, so a design company is doing a new company logo for us. We're also reorganising the sales office. We've had problems there.
- And are you doing anything about your old computer system?
- Yes, a company called Tabcom is upgrading our virus protection software. Do you know Tabcom?
- No, I don't. Are they good?
- Yes, they're very good. As I said, they're installing the system and preparing all the software. They're also reorganising our data storage for us.
- It's a lot of work.
- Yes, it is. And we've decided to redecorate the reception area and showroom.
- Who is doing that?
- We're doing it ourselves. Our maintenance people are doing it.
- It's quite a big project.

- Yes …
- Good luck with it.

UNIT 27 Shopping
1 Key dialogues

a
- Can I help you?
- Yes, please. I'm looking for a winter coat.
- Do you know your size?
- Yes, it's 40.
- Do you know what that is in a European size?
- No, I'm afraid I don't.

b
- Have you got any of these shirts in blue?
- Yes, we have.
- And have you got them in a bigger size?
- No, I'm afraid we haven't.
- That's a shame.

c
- Can I try these trousers on?
- Yes, of course. The fitting room's over there.
- They fit, but they don't suit me.
- Try these. They might be better. Yes, they're much better. They suit you, and they fit you very well.

d
- Excuse me, can you help me? I'm looking for a gift for my wife.
- Certainly, how about some perfume?
- That's a good idea. Where can I find perfume?
- It's in the cosmetics department on the first floor.

3 Listening

- Can I have two 35mm films, please? How much are they?
- Six euros each.
- Can I pay in American dollars?
- No, I'm sorry, we only take euros.
- And how much are the American newspapers?
- Four euros.
- And what soft drinks have you got?
- Coke and Sprite. The drinks are two euros fifty each.
- OK. Can I have a paper and a Coke, and two stamps for the USA please?
- So that's four euros for the paper, two euros fifty for the Coke, and two euros twenty for the stamps. Oh yes, and twelve euros for the two films. That comes to twenty euros and seventy cents.
- Those key rings look interesting. How much are they?
- Four fifty each.

UNIT 28 Your colleagues
1 Key dialogues

a
- What does your boss look like?
- He's tall with glasses.
- Which one is he?
- He's the one wearing a blue suit.
- Is that his wife?
- He isn't married.

b
- Who's that woman over there?
- Which one?
- The one in the green dress, with dark hair.
- She's our sales director.
- Is she new?
- No, she's been with the company for years.

c – Is that your new assistant?
  – Where?
  – The one with the fair hair.
  – Yes.
  – Does he have a family?
  – I don't think so. He's divorced.

d – Is that your CEO?
  – Yes, it is.
  – He looks young.
  – He isn't really. He's been with the company for over twenty years.
  – What's he like?
  – He's very nice.
  – Is he a good boss?
  – I think so, but I don't work with him.

4 Listening
Dialogue 1
– The blonde woman on the left with glasses is Nina Luoti.
– What does she do?
– She's the production supervisor on the project.
– She looks young – how old is she?
– I don't know – she's married with two children.
– How long's she been with the company?
– About eighteen months.

Dialogue 2
– Who's Ken Bruger?
– He's from KC Supplies.
– Which one is he?
– He's the one on the left with dark hair and a grey suit.
– Do you know him?
– I know he's their European Sales Manager. He lives in Frankfurt. He's married with a young baby.

UNIT 29 Your office building
1 Key dialogues

a – Good morning, my name is Libi Yusri. I have an appointment with Mr Guala.
  – Could you sign in, please? If you take the lift to the second floor, he'll meet you at the lift.
  – Thank you. Where's the lift?
  – Over there. This is your security pass.

b – Excuse me, is the training department this way?
  – No, it's not on this floor. Go to the lift and go to the seventh floor. When you come out of the lift, turn right – it's at the end of the corridor on the right.
  – Thanks.

c – Is the boardroom on this floor?
  – Yes, it is. Go along this corridor, and through the double doors. It's the last door on the left. It's not far.
  – Can I get through OK? I don't have a swipe card.
  – Yes, press the green button and someone will open the door.

d – Can I help you?
  – Yes, I'm looking for Meeting Room 3.
  – It's not this floor. I think you're in the wrong building.
  – Reception said it was on the fifth floor.
  – Ah, this is the fourth floor.

3 Listening
Dialogue 1
A: Good morning. My name's Nancy Lee. I'm from Link International and I have an appointment with Mr Irwin.
B: Good morning, Ms Lee. is that L-double E?
A: Yes, it is.
B: Ah yes, Mr Irwin is expecting you. Could you sign in, please …? (Picks up phone) Mr Irwin? Oh … this is Reception. We have Nancy Lee from Link International – she has an appointment with Mr Irwin. Right. Thank you. (Puts phone down)
A: Where is the training department?
B: It's on the second floor. If you take the lift over there to the second floor, they'll meet you.
A: Thank you.
B: Miss Lee, don't forget your security pass.
A: Oh …

Dialogue 2
C: Excuse me, my name is Paul Ansah. I'm from Phototex. I have an appointment with your HR department. Which way is it?
D: I'll check. Can you fill in the visitor's book please? Where's the HR department.
A: It's above Maintenance.
D: Oh yes, thanks. I'm sorry, I'm new here. Who are you seeing?
C: I'm not sure – I'm doing a presentation. It's organised by Jo Lake.
D: Jo Lake – let me check for you. (Picks up phone) Is that Jo Lake? This is Reception. We have Mr Ansah. He's from Phototex. Right. OK. Thanks. (Puts phone down) Mr Ansah, Jo Lake is waiting for you. Could you take the lift to the first floor? When you come out of the lift, turn left and follow the corridor to the left. The HR department is the second door on the left. There's a card swipe on the left – press the green button.
C: Thanks.
D: This is your security pass.

UNIT 30 How things work
1 Key dialogues

a – Excuse me, how do you start this DVD player?
  – You press the start button.
  – I did that.
  – Did you turn it on?
  – Yes, I did.
  – Is it plugged in?
  – No, but it's got a battery.

b – I don't know how this works, do you?
  – To start it, you press the green button. To stop it, you press the red one.
  – Thanks very much.

c – Do you know how to use this?
  – I'm not sure.
  – Does it usually make that noise?
  – I don't think so. Aren't there any instructions?
  – No, I can't see any.
  – I think the paper is jammed.

d – I think there's a problem with my computer. I can't access my files.
   – No, it's not your computer. The server's down. We're fixing it but I'm afraid it'll take a while.

3 Listening

Dialogue 1
– Do you know how to work this digital camera?
– No, I don't. Where are the instructions?
– Here.
– It says if it doesn't work, check that it's charged. Is the battery charged?
– I don't think so.
– OK, is it plugged in?
– Yes.
– I think it takes about an hour to charge.

Dialogue 2
– I don't know how this shredder works. Do you know how to use it?
– Yes, I think so.
– Does it always stop like that?
– No …
– What does that light mean?
– I think it means the paper's jammed. Where are the instructions?
– Here …
– It says you must feed it a maximum of five sheets at a time.

UNIT 31 Requesting information
1 Key dialogues

a – Could you give me the reference number?
   – It's FC 4000X.
   – That one is available in two sizes, standard and large.
   – What's it made of?
   – It's made of metal.
   – Thanks, I'll get back to you.

b – Do you have the model number?
   – Yes, it's ELC 901K.
   – Right, how can I help you?
   – Is it available in grey?
   – I'll just check.

c – Yes, we have that desk in stock.
   – How big is it?
   – It's two metres eighty by ninety-five centimetres.
   – Thanks, is it possible to order on-line?
   – Yes. Go to our website – the address is officefurniture dot com. Click on 'buy on-line'.

d – The standard model is out of stock, but we have the large model.
   – Do you have it in brown?
   – No, it comes in black or white.
   – Do you deliver?
   – Yes, takes three days.
   – OK, I'd like to order a large white one.

3 Listening

– Could I have some information about one of your filing cabinets, please?
– Can you give me the model number, please?

– It's FC 203XJ.
– Right, how can I help you?
– Could you tell me how big it is?
– It comes in three sizes: large, medium and small.
– How big is the medium one?
– It's forty-six centimetres by sixty-five centimetres by one metre thirty.
– What colour is it?
– It's available in three colours: grey, blue and red. The red one is out of stock at the moment.
– And how much is it?
– The range is on special offer – the medium size is sixty-three euros.
– Does that include delivery?
– It depends – we don't charge for delivery on orders over a hundred euros.
– OK – I'd like to order the medium, in grey.
– And how many do you want?
– Five.
– OK. So, I need your delivery details.

UNIT 32 Staying in a hotel
1 Key dialogues

a – I'd like to book a room, please.
   – When is it for, madam?
   – Next weekend. I need a double room with a balcony.
   – I'm afraid we're full then.
   – Oh, what a pity!
   – I'm sorry, but it's so busy at the moment.

b – Good evening, sir.
   – Good evening. We'd like a room, please.
   – Do you have a reservation?
   – Ah, no, we don't.
   – How many nights is it for?
   – Just tonight.

c – Can we book on-line?
   – Yes, just go to our website and click on 'reservations'.
   – Thanks.

d – A single room with a bathroom …
   – That's fine. What name is it, please?
   – Dashti.
   – How do you spell that?
   – D-A-S-H-T-I.
   – Could you fill in this card please? Would you like someone to take your bag?
   – No, that's OK. I can carry it myself.

4 Listening

Call 1
– I'd like a room, please.
– Is it for tonight?
– Yes, it is.
– A single or a double?
– A double. We'd like it for five nights. Is … is that possible?
– Yes, that's fine. What name is it, please?
– Mistri. That's M-I-S-T-R-I.
– Thank you, sir. Now, can you fill in this card, please?
– Sure. The room has a bathroom, doesn't it?
– Yes, it does.

Call 2
- This is YZ Chemicals. I'd like to book a room for our sales Manager, Mr Yusufzai.
- When does he want the room?
- From the night of the 12th.
- I'm afraid we're full up on the 12th.
- How about the following week, the 19th?
- Does he want a single or a double?
- A double with bathroom.
- All our rooms have en suite bathrooms. And how many nights is it for?
- Three. Is that OK?
- Yes, that'll be fine. What was the name?
- Yusufzai.
- I'm sorry. Could you spell that …?
- Y-U-S-U-F-Z-A-I.

UNIT 33 Booking conference facilities
1 Key dialogues

a - We're looking for a room for a conference.
- When is it?
- On the 25th.
- How big is the conference?
- We're expecting between fifteen and twenty delegates.

b - Is the room big enough? It's about eighteen metres long.
- That's fine. How much do you charge?
- That room is two thousand euros a day.
- Does that include coffee?
- No, refreshments are extra?

c - Do you want it all day?
- No, just from nine o'clock till lunchtime.
- Conference Room B is available. It's eleven metres long and seven metres wide.
- No, I think that's too small.

d - How many people is it for?
- Nine or ten.
- What about the Rothschild Room?
- It's too big. Have you got anything smaller?
- You could use the JP Morgan Suite.
- How much is it?
- It's five hundred euros an hour.
- OK, I'd like to book it. Do you supply AV equipment?
- Yes, we do.

4 Listening

- We're looking for a conference room for the 5th of this month.
- How many people is it for?
- About eighty.
- Conference Room B is available, but I don't think it's big enough.
- How big is it?
- It's about fifteen metres long.
- And how wide?
- About nine metres.
- I think it's too small. Have you got anything bigger?
- Yes, but it's not available. Conference Room A is twenty-one metres long, but it's booked till the 11th. Then it's available till the 21st.

- What about parking?
- That's no problem – we have a car park in the basement.
- OK. How much is Room A?
- It's two thousand five hundred euros per day.
- Does that include refreshments?
- It includes tea and coffee, but not lunch.
- And how much do you charge for lunch?
- Our finger buffet is twenty-five euros per head.
- OK, I'll get back to you. Thanks.

UNIT 34 Organising a trip
1 Key dialogues

a - I'd like a return ticket to Bahrain.
- When do you want to travel?
- On Thursday the 19th.
- Business or economy class?
- Business, please.
- There's a Continental Airlines flight at 09.30. It arrives in Bahrain at 16.00 hours.

b - Is there a quicker way?
- You could take an internal flight but the train is more convenient. It goes to the centre of Paris.
- When does the plane arrive?
- At 9.40. But then you'd need to travel into Paris.

c - I'd like a first class return to Barbados.
- When do you want to travel?
- Tomorrow.
- Okay, I'll call you when the seats are booked.
- How much is it going to cost?
- Around four thousand dollars.

d - There are two flights tomorrow: one at 11.00 hours and one at 14.05.
- When does the 14.05 flight arrive?
- At 17.40. Shall I book it?
- Yes, please.
- I'll email you when I have the details.

3 Listening

- I have the details of your booking. Can I check them with you?
- Yes, go ahead.
- You leave London Heathrow on 18th June at 10.20. You're flying with Continental Airways, flight number CA 216.
- CA 216.
- I'll email the itinerary and the ticket reference number.
- Oh, thanks.
- Your flight arrives in Manila at 13.40 on the 19th.
- That's fine.
- You leave for Djakarta on the 24th, flying by Continental Airways, flight number CA 320.
- What time is that?
- You depart at 16.15 and arrive in Djakarta at 19.10. Is that OK?
- Yes, that's very good.
- OK. The flight from Djakarta to Bangkok is on the 27th at 09.45, flight number TP 190. That's Trans Pacific.
- How many days do I have in Bangkok?

- Three. You leave on the 30th of June on the 22.30 flight – CA 820. That's Continental Airways again. And that arrives in London at 08.35 on the 1st of July.
- That's fine.
- Shall I confirm the bookings?
- Yes, go ahead.

UNIT 35 Hiring a car

1 Key dialogues

a
- Where can I hire a car?
- There's a place inside the airport?
- Are their prices reasonable?
- Well, something like a Corolla Estate costs about four hundred and eighty pounds a week.
- That sounds expensive!

b
- That car might suit you.
- What make is it?
- It's a Renault.
- And how much is it?
- Five hundred and fifty dollars per week.
- Does that include insurance?
- It includes insurance and unlimited mileage.
- That seems OK.

c
- What kind of car do you want?
- I'm looking for something like a Volvo estate.
- We have a Mercedes estate that might suit you.
- Can I book on-line?
- Yes, of course.

d
- When do you want the car?
- This Monday.
- And how long do you want it for?
- A week to ten days.
- So I need your credit card details

3 Listening

- I want to hire a car, please.
- Certainly, sir. When do you want it?
- Next Wednesday.
- That's the 22nd of July. And how long do you want it for?
- A week.
- Right. What size car do you want?
- Something like a VW Passat.
- We haven't got a Passat. We have a Toyota that might suit you …
- Which model is it?
- It's a Corolla GL five-door hatchback.
- What colour is it?
- It's silver – and it's this year's model. It is fitted with GPS.
- How much is it?
- It's five hundred dollars per week.
- That seems a bit expensive.
- The rental includes insurance, tax and unlimited mileage.
- OK, I'll take it.
- So, I need your credit card details.
- OK.
- When you collect the car, you will need to have your credit card and passport with you.
- Right.
- And you will need to sign the rental agreement.

- But the car is booked …
- Yes, what time will you pick it up?

UNIT 36 Returning home

1 Key dialogues

a
- Welcome back – how was your trip?
- It went well. I saw most of the people I needed to see. There was a lot of interest in our new products.
- Well done – when did you get back?
- This morning.

b
- It is good to be back.
- How's Dick?
- He's well. He sent you his regards. He says the new ordering system won't work in his market.
- We need to debrief.
- My report will be ready tomorrow.

c
- There was a lot of interest.
- But you didn't get any firm orders?
- I'm afraid not.
- And the problem is delivery times?
- I'm afraid so.

d
- I was booked to fly on Monday, but my manager wanted me to come back early. I managed to change the flight to Sunday morning instead.
- Did you have to pay extra.
- Yes, I had to upgrade to first class.

e
- I needed more time in Lima.
- Were you able to reschedule?
- Yes, the airline was very helpful. I had to pay a small supplement – that's all.

4 Listening

- Hi Joe. I didn't know you were back.
- Yes, I got back this morning. I was booked to fly on Thursday but I got a call from my wife asking me to come home early. It's my daughter's birthday tomorrow. So I rescheduled and came home today instead. Luckily I managed to get a flight.
- Did you have to pay extra?
- Yes, I had to upgrade to first – but I think it will be OK if I pay the difference myself.
- It's good to have you back.
- It's good to be back. Oh, Mia sends you her regards.
- How is she?
- She's well – very busy.
- Is the programme on schedule?
- I'm afraid not. There are problems with the new IT system. We need to talk.
- When will your report be ready.
- Tomorrow morning.
- So let's talk tomorrow.
- It will have to be in the morning, I'm out in the afternoon for my daughter's birthday outing.
- OK. Oh, and Joe … welcome back.

List of irregular verbs

Infinitive	Past Tense	Past Participle	Infinitive	Past Tense	Past Participle
be	was/were	been	leave	left	left
bear	bore	born	lend	lent	lent
begin	began	begun	let	let	let
break	broke	broken	lose	lost	lost
bring	brought	brought	make	made	made
build	built	built	mean	meant	meant
burn	burnt/burned	burnt/burned	meet	met	met
buy	bought	bought	pay	paid	paid
catch	caught	caught	put	put	put
choose	chose	chosen	read	read	read
come	came	come	ride	rode	ridden
cost	cost	cost	ring	rang	rung
cut	cut	cut	run	ran	run
deal	dealt	dealt	say	said	said
do	did	done	see	saw	seen
drink	drank	drunk	sell	sold	sold
drive	drove	driven	send	sent	sent
eat	ate	eaten	set	set	set
fall	fell	fallen	show	showed	shown
feed	fed	fed	shut	shut	shut
feel	felt	felt	sit	sat	sat
find	found	found	sleep	slept	slept
fly	flew	flown	speak	spoke	spoken
forget	forgot	forgotten	spell	spelt	spelt
get	got	got (US gotten)	spend	spent	spent
give	gave	given	stand	stood	stood
go	went	gone	swim	swam	swum
grow	grew	grown	take	took	taken
have	had	had	teach	taught	taught
hear	heard	heard	tell	told	told
hold	held	held	think	thought	thought
hurt	hurt	hurt	understand	understood	understood
keep	kept	kept	wear	wore	worn
know	knew	known	win	won	won
lead	led	led	write	wrote	written
learn	learnt	learnt			

Grammar/language index

Word list

A

a (1)
about (5) *about five kilometres west of the city*
about (5) *How about …? What about …?*
about (13) *I'm calling about the meeting.*
about (18) *at about nine*
above (29) *The office is above here.*
accept (25)
accounts (2)
accountant (1)
address (1)
admin = administration (6)
advertising manager (2)
afraid (10) *I'm afraid I can't make it.*
after (12)
afternoon (7)
again (8)
agent (5)
ago (21)
ahead (11) *go ahead*
airport (3)
aisle (25)
along (6)
all (7)
all right (22)
always (30)
am (1)
American (1)
an (1)
and (3)
another (13)
answer (18)
any (3)
anyone (26)
anything (8)
April (9)
are (1)
area (6) *testing area*
aren't = are not (1)
around (18) *at around ten*
arrangements (7)
arrivals hall (22)
arrive (23)
as good as (20)
ask (17)
assistant (2) *assistant sales manager*
at (9) *at Christmas*
at (10) *at four o'clock*
at (18) *at about ten o'clock*
at (18) *at around nine o'clock*
at (29) *at home, the station, the end of, etc.*
August (9)
aunt (14)
Australia (4)
autumn (9)
AV equipment (33)
available (31)
avenue (3)
away (5) *two kilometres away*

away (12) *I'll be away*
awful (7)

B

back (12) *be back before five be back from Paris*
back to (29) *go back to the lift*
bad (8) *not too bad bad line*
bag (22)
Bahrain (34)
bald (28)
bank (2)
bars (3)
basement (3)
bath (32)
bathroom (32)
be (1)
beamer (33)
beautiful (21)
because (12)
bedroom (32)
beef (20)
been (21) *Have you been here before?*
before (12)
begin (12)
behind (6)
believe (8)
below (29)
Berlin (1)
better (13)
big (5)
bill (20)
biscuit (19)
black (19)
block (6) *main block*
blue (27)
boardroom (12)
boarding pass (22)
book (32)
booked (12)
booking (36)
borrow (26)
boss (13)
bottle (20)
bottom (29) *at the bottom of the stairs*
box (20)
Brazil (7)
Brazilian (7)
briefcase (22)
Britain (7)
brochure (31)
broken (23)
brother (14)
building (3)
bunch (20)
bus (23)
bus service (23)
business (4) *in the insurance business*
busy (13)
but (3)

button (30)
buy (4)
by (12) *back by two*
by (29) *His office is by reception.*
by (31) *1 metre 20 by 90 centimetres*
bye (9)

C

cafes (3)
cake (20) *a piece of cake*
cakes (19)
call (9)
call (18) *make a call*
call off (13)
caller (16)
called (2)
cancel (13)
can (10) *can't = cannot*
canteen (3)
carafe (20)
card (1)
car (92)
car industry (4)
car park (3)
cars (4)
carry (32)
cases (22)
catch (16) *I didn't catch your name*
catch the bus (26
catering (29)
centimetre (31)
centre (3)
centre (6) *conference centre*
CEO = chief executive officer (28)
certainly (18)
chair (31)
chairman (2)
chairperson (2)
change (12) *change the time of the meeting*
change (14) *I didn't have any change.*
charge (33)
cheap (20)
check (11)
check in (22)
check-in desk (22)
cheers (20)
chicken (20)
children (28)
China (7)
Chinese (7)
chocolate (19)
Christmas (9)
church (21)
cinema (21)
city (5)
clear customs (22)
client (14)
close (26)
coat (22)
coffee (3)
coffee machine (3)

cold (14)
colour (31)
come (8)
come in (9)
company (1)
computer (4, 26)
conference (10)
conference centre (6)
confirm (11)
contact (18)
continental size (27)
convenient (21)
corridor (6)
cost (34)
cough (14)
could (11) *Could you let me know?*
country (5)
cream (19)
credit card (27)
cup, cups (3)
cup (20) *a cup of tea*
customer (16)
customs (22)

D
dark (28)
data processing (29)
date (10)
daughter (14)
days (8)
deadline (13)
dear (7) *Oh dear …*
December (9)
degrees (24)
delayed (24)
delegates (33)
delicious (19)
deliver (31)
delivery (31)
depart (22) *What platform does the train depart from*
department (1)
departures hall (22)
deputy (2) *deputy sales director*
desk (17)
dessert (20)
details (11)
develop (4)
dial (18)
diary (11)
did (14) *didn't = did not*
director (2) *finance director*
distributors (5)
division (2) *sales division*
divorced (28)
do (1) *What do you do?*
do business (4)
doctor (14)
does (2) *Does she like her job?*
dollars (17, 23)
don't = do not (2)
door (6)
double room (32)
down (6)
down to (29)

downstairs (6)
dress (28)
drink (19)
drive (3)
drive up (6) *drive up there*
driving licence (35)
dry (20)
due (23)

E
each (27)
earlier (12)
east (5)
Easter (9)
Eastern Europe (4)
easy (20)
eat (19)
economy class (34)
Edinburgh (24)
Egypt (7)
Egyptian (7)
eight (3)
eighteen (3)
eighth (3)
eighty (3)
either (13)
electrical engineer (2)
eleven (3)
else (19) *anything else*
email (18)
end (16) *until the end of the week*
end (29) *at the end of the corridor*
engaged (18)
engineer (1)
engineering (1) *AB Engineering*
England (7)
English (7)
enjoy (20)
enjoy (25) *We enjoyed having you here.*
enough (23)
entrance (6)
estate (35)
euro (17)
evening (7)
ever (21)
everything (9)
exactly (5)
excellent (3)
excuse me (1)
executive (31)
expect (23)
expensive (20)
export (4)
extension 123 (15)
extension lead (26)
extra (33)

F
factory (93)
fair (28)
fall (US) = autumn (9)
family (8)
far (3) *not far*
far (29) *How far?*
Far East (4)

fare (23)
father (14)
faulty (30)
fax (18)
fax (26)
February (9)
ferry (34)
festival (21)
few (7) *a few words*
fifteen (3)
fifth (3)
fifty (3)
files (19)
filing cabinet (31)
fill in (35)
finance (1) *finance department*
find (6)
find out (12)
fine (7)
finish (14)
firm (2)
first (3)
first (30) *First …, then …*
first floor (3)
first name (1)
fish (20)
fit (27)
fitting room (27)
five (3)
flight (7)
flipchart (26)
floor (3)
flowers (20)
fly (8)
food (20)
follow (23)
football match (21)
for (1) *work for*
for (8) *for five days*
forget (9)
form (35)
four (3)
fourteen (3)
fourth (3)
forty (3)
France (4)
francs (17)
free (10)
free time (21)
freezing (24)
French (7)
Friday (8)
from (1)
fruit (20)
frustrating (32)
full (32)
fully booked (36)
fuse (30)

G
games (4) *computer games*
gate (6) *main gate, gate number*
gentleman (29)
German (12)
get (19)

get back (31)
get into (23)
get through (18)
gift (25)
give (9)
glad (25)
glasses (28) *the tall one with glasses*
go (4) *Is business going well?*
go (6) *go down there*
go ahead (11)
go through (24)
going to (13) *going to be busy*
good (3)
good afternoon (7)
goodbye (9)
good evening (7)
good morning (1)
goods inwards (6)
green (28)
Greek (12)
grey (28)
ground floor (29)

H
hair (28)
half an hour = 30 minutes (23)
half past three = 3.30 (16)
hand luggage (22)
happen (14)
has (3)
have (3) *haven't = have not*
have got (14) *I've got a cold.*
have got (23) *We'll have to start earlier.*
he (1) *he's = he is*
he's got = he has got (14)
head office (4)
hear (8)
Help Desk (6, 26)
her (2) *I don't know her.*
her (5) *her car*
here (1)
hers (19) *It's hers.*
herself (32)
hello (7)
help (27)
his (7)
him (2)
himself (32)
hire (35)
his (19) *It's his.*
hold on (15)
hole punch (26)
holiday (16)
home (8)
home number (1)
hope (25)
hospital (14)
host (19)
hotel (7)
hours (7)
how (2)
how do you do (7)
hundred (3)
Hungary (7)
Hungarian (7)

hungry (19)
hurry (22)
husband (14)

I
I (1)
I'd = I would (7)
idea (3)
ill (13)
I'll = I will (9)
I'm = I am (1)
import (4)
important (13)
in (1) *in finance, in London*
in (6) *in that building*
in (10) *in the afternoon*
include (20)
Independence Day (9)
India (4)
India (20)
Indian (20)
Indonesian (20)
industry (4) *in the car industry*
info = information (15)
information system (4)
in front of (6)
in order to (11)
inside (35)
instructions (30)
insurance (2)
instead (36) *on Monday instead, on Monday instead of Tuesday*
interested in (15)
interesting (21)
into (29)
irritating (32)
is (1) *isn't = is not*
it (1) *it's = it is*
it (2) *I like it.*
Italian (1)
itinerary (24)
its (5)
itself (32)
I've got = I have got (14)

J
January (9)
Japan (7)
Japanese (7)
job (2)
join (28)
journey (7)
July (9)
June (9)
just (18) *just after/before*
just (24) *My car's just over there.*

K
keep in touch (9)
keys (35)
keyboard (26)
kilometres (5)
kind (25)
kitchen (29)

know (2)
Korea (5)

L
ladies (29)
land (23)
large (31)
last (14) *last week*
last (29) *last door on the right*
late (7)
later (12)
law firm (2)
lawyer (2)
leave (8)
leave a message (18)
left (6) *on the left of*
leg room (23)
legal (29)
lend (26)
less (36)
let me know (11)
let's (12)
licence (35) *driving licence*
life (8)
lift (29) *Take the lift to the seventh floor.*
like (2) *I like my job.*
like (7) *I'd like to welcome you.*
like (24) *I like working here.*
like (35) *something like a Volvo*
line (18)
Lisbon (34)
litre (22)
little (7) *a little English*
lobby (32)
London (1)
long (8) *How long are you here for?*
look (26)
looks (35) *looks expensive*
look after (25)
look for (29)
lot (4) *a lot of*
lose (14)
love (25) *I love eating out.*
low (20)
luggage (22)
lunch (3, 33)
lunch date (13)
lunchtime (24)

M
made of (31)
magazine (23)
main market (4)
main office (5)
main gate (6)
main course (20)
maintenance block (6)
make (4) *make shoes*
make (4) *make a profit*
make (10) *make the meeting*
make (18) *make a call*
make (30) *make a noise*
make (35) *What make is the car?*
Malacca (5)
Malaysia (5)

Malaysian ringgit (17)
manage (22)
manager (1)
management information system (4)
managing director (2)
manufacturing (2)
many (4)
March (9)
marketing (29)
markets (4)
married (28)
may (27)
May (9)
MD = managing director (9)
me (2)
meal (20)
medical (29) *medical unit*
medium (31)
meet (1)
meeting (10)
mend (26)
menu (20)
message (16)
metal (31)
metre (31)
Mexican (20)
Middle East (4)
might (27)
mileage (35)
milk (3)
millions (17)
mine (19)
minutes (23)
Miss (2)
miss (14)
mm (19) *Mm, they're delicious.*
mobile number (1)
model (35) *What model is the car?*
model number (31)
modern (21)
moment (4) *at the moment*
moment (15) *just a moment, one moment*
money (4) *make money*
Monday (8)
more (19) *more expensive than*
morning (1)
Moscow (34)
most (21) *the most interesting part of town*
mother (14)
move (23)
Mr (2)
Mrs (2)
Ms (2)
much (2)
much (22) *How much?*
mug (20)
must (3)
must (9) *You must visit us again soon.*
my (2)
myself (32)

N
name (1)
nationality (1)
near (3)
nearby (3)
need (22)
never (28)
new (4) *new product*
New Year (9)
New York (8)
newspaper (23)
next (9)
next to (6)
next week (9)
nice (1)
night (32)
nine (3)
nineteen (3)
ninety (3)
ninth (3)
no (1)
noise (30)
non-smoking (22)
normally (30)
north (5)
North Africa (4)
north-east (5)
north-west (5)
not (1)
not at all (9)
nothing (9) *It's nothing.*
November (9)
now (15)
nuisance (32)
number (1)

O
occupation (1)
occupied (12)
o'clock (10) *four o'clock*
October (9)
of (3) *centre of town*
of course (17)
offer (19)
office (2)
often (30)
oh (7) *oh good, oh dear*
OHP = overhead projector (26)
OK (2)
old (21)
on (2) *on the sales side*
on (6) *on the left*
on (7) *on time*
on to (29)
one (2) *Which ones?*
one (3)
one (10) *one Saturday*
one way (34)
ones (19)
online (31)
open (25)
opera (21)
opposite (6)
order (11) *in order to*
order (31)

organise (25)
other (5)
out (16)
out of (29)
out of order (18)
our (5)
ours (19)
ourselves (32)
outside (23)
over (6) *over there*

P
pack (22)
paint shop (6)
parcel (4)
part (21)
part time (5)
parts (4)
pass on (25)
passport (22)
past (6)
path (6)
pay (27)
payphone (18)
PCs = personal computers (24)
pen (26)
people (4)
pesos (17)
per cent = % (4)
perhaps (26)
personnel (1) *personnel department*
phone (11)
photo (5)
photocopier (26)
piece (20) *a piece of cake*
pint (20) *a pint of beer*
pity (32)
place (5)
plane = aeroplane (US airplane) (7)
plants (5)
plastic (31)
plates (19)
please (15)
pleased (7)
pleasure (9) *It's my pleasure.*
plenty (23)
plug (30)
plug in (30)
pork (20)
possible (15)
post (32)
postpone (13)
postroom (29)
potatoes (20) *french fried, boiled*
pounds (17)
PR = Public Relations (7)
price (17)
present (27)
presentation (26)
press (30)
problem (12)
process manager (2)
product (4)
production (28)

production manager (2)
production plants (5)
profit (4) *make a profit*
programme (24)
pronounce (34)
purchasing (29)
put off (13)
put through (15)

Q
a quarter of an hour = 15 minutes (23)
a quarter past three = 3.15 (16)
a quarter to four = 3.45 (16)
quicker (34)
quite (4)

R
raining (24)
R&D = Research and Development (2)
ready (13)
reasonable (35)
receive (25)
reception (29)
reception area (3)
recommend (20)
recorder (26)
records (29)
recruitment (29)
red (30)
reference number (31)
regards (9)
remember me to (9)
remind (11)
rep = representative (1)
repeat (15)
report (2, 31)
reserve(d) (12, 32)
reservation (32)
restaurants (3)
return ticket (34)
right (6) *on the right of*
right (8) *That's right.*
ring (17)
road (3)
room (23) *leg room*
room (32) *room number*
round (29) *Follow the corridor round to the left.*
rouble (17)
rupees (17)
Russia (4)

S
Saigon (5)
salad (20)
sales (1) *sales department*
sales (1) *sales manager*
sales (1) *sales rep*
sales (2) *sales division*
sales (2) *sales staff*
sales (28) *sales director*
salmon (20)
sandwich (19)
Saturday (8)

saucer, saucers (3)
Saudi riyal (17)
say (17)
scanner (26)
school (14)
screen (33)
seat (22)
seat belt (23)
second (3)
secretary (13)
section (2) *the sales section*
see (7)
seems (35)
see you (9)
sell (4)
seminar (26)
send (4)
separated (28)
September (9)
serve (23)
service (6, 20)
seven (3)
seventeen (3)
seventh (3)
seventy (3)
she (1) *she's = she is*
shall (19)
shining (24)
shirts (27)
shoes (4)
shops (3)
shopping centre (21)
short (19) *short break*
show (30)
show round (25)
showroom (6)
shredder (26, 30)
side (2) *on the sales side*
sign (27)
signs (21)
single (28)
single room (32)
single ticket (34)
sister (14)
sitting-room (32)
six (3)
sixteen (3)
sixth (3)
sixty (3)
size (27)
small (4)
smoking (22)
snow (24)
snowing (24)
so (25) *so did I*
so (32) *so busy*
software (4)
some (3)
someone (26)
something (19)
sometimes (30)
son (14)
sore throat (14)
sorry (14, 15)
sounds (26)

soup (20)
source (33)
south (5)
south-east (5)
South-East Asia (4)
south-west (5)
Spain (7)
Spanish (7)
speak (7)
speak up (18)
spell (2)
spring (9)
stairs (29)
standard (31)
stapler (26)
start (12)
starter (20)
(the) States = the USA (7)
station (3)
stay (21)
steak (20)
stewardess (23)
still (11)
stock (31) *in stock, out of stock*
stop (23) *bus stop*
stop (30)
storeroom (29)
stores (6)
straight on (6)
street (3)
such (32) *such a busy time*
sugar (3)
suitcase (22)
suit (27) *The trousers don't suit me.*
suits (13) *That time suits me.*
summer (9)
support (18) *IT support*
Sunday (8)
supplement (36)
sure (17)
surname (1)
surprise (25)
Sweden (34)
swipe card (29)
switch on (30)
switch (30)
system (4) *management information system*

T
take (14)
take off (23)
talk (16)
tall (28)
tea (3)
telephone number (1)
tell (17)
temperature (24)
ten (3)
tenth (3)
terminal (23)
terrible (7)
testing area (6)
Thai (20)
Thailand (5)
than (20) *better than*

thanks (9)
thanks (11) *Thanks for calling.*
thank you (9)
thank you (25) *thank you very much indeed*
that (6)
the (2)
theatre (21)
their (5)
theirs (19)
them (2)
themselves (32)
then (12) *I can't make it then.*
then (30) *first ..., then ...*
there is/are (3)
there (5) *We have two offices there.*
these (6)
they (1)
think (28)
think so (28)
third (3)
thirteen (3)
thirty (3)
this (6)
those (6)
thousand (5)
three (3)
three-quarters (23) *three-quarters of an hour*
throat (14)
through (6) *Go through reception.*
through flight (22)
Thursday (8)
tickets (21)
till (10)
time (7) *on time*
time (10) *What time?*
time (11) *Can I check the time?*
timetable (24)
today (10)
to (1) *to meet*
to (5) *to the south*
to (6) *walk to the top*
to (11) *I'm calling to confirm Tuesday's meeting.*
toilet (6)
Tokyo (22)
tomorrow (8)
tonight (32)
too (7)
toothache (14)
top (29) *at the top of the stairs*
town (3)
traditional (25)
training (6)
trains (7)
trousers (14, 27)
try on (27)
Tuesday (8)
turn (6)
turn on (30)
twelve (3)
twenty, twenty-one, etc. (3)
two (3)
type (26)

U

(the) United States (7)
uncle (14)
understand (8)
unit (29) *medical unit*
unlimited mileage (35)
until (13)
unusual (21)
up (6)
up to (29)
upstairs (6)
urgent (13)
us (2)
use (18) *use the phone*
usually (30)

V

vacancies (32)
VAT = value-added tax (20)
veal (20)
vegetables (20)
very (2)
video (26)
village (5)
virus (26) *virus protection software*
visit (8)
visitor (20)
vodka (26)

W

wait for (4)
waiter (20)
waitress (20)
walk (6)
want (32)
warehouse (3, 6)
was (7) *wasn't = was not*
way (6) *this way, that way*
way (34) *It's £600 one way.*
we (1) *we're = we are*
wear (28)
wearing (28)
weather (7)
Wednesday (8)
week (9)
weekend (32)
welcome (7) *welcome to, welcome back*
welcome (9) *You're welcome.*
well (2)
were (7) *weren't = were not*
west (5) *west of the city*
Western Europe (4)
what (1)
when (8)
when (34) *I'll contact you when I have the tickets.*
where (1)
whereabouts (5)
which (2)
whisky (23)
white (19)
who (1)
whose (19)
why (7)
wide (33)

wife (9)
will (9) *I'll call you next week. I'll have the beef.* (20)
window seat (22)
wine (20)
winter (9)
with (19)
without (19)
wonderful (25)
won't = will not (9) *I won't forget.*
wood (31)
words (7)
work (2)
work for (1)
work number (1)
work on (4) *We're working on a new product.*
workshop (6)
worry (14)
worried (24)
worse (20)
wrap (27)
write (11)
wrong (13) *What's wrong?*
would (19) *Would you like a coffee?*
would (34) *It would be cheaper.*

Y

year (9)
year (35) *What year is the car?*
six years old (27) *a six year-old child*
yen (17)
yes (1)
yesterday (14)
yet (11)
you (1)
young (28)
your (5)
yours (19)
yourself (22)
yourselves (32)
yuan (17)

Glossary of business-related terms

accountant: 1 person who keeps a company's accounts
2 person who advises a company on its finances

accounts: 1 record of transactions over a period of time
2 department in a company which deals with money paid, received, borrowed or owed

admin: administration

administration: organisation or control or management of a company, e.g. sales administration

advertising: business of announcing that something is for sale or of trying to persuade customers to buy a product or service, e.g. advertising department

advice note: written notice to a customer giving details of goods ordered and shipped but not yet delivered

air freight: method of shipping goods in an aircraft

assembly plant: factory where cars are put together from parts made in other factories

asset: thing which belongs to a company or person, and which has a value

associate: 1 connected in some way, e.g. an associate company, 'XYZ Associates'
2 person who works in the same business as someone, e.g. a business associate

audit: examination of the books and accounts of a company

auditor: company or person who audits the books and accounts, usually an external firm of accountants

balance: amount remaining, e.g. *I'll pay the balance next week*

balance sheet: statement of the financial position of a company at a particular time

bank transfer: moving money from one bank account to another account

beamer: see digital projector

bleeper: a small portable device with a screen which enables the user to receive short messages

board: group of people who run an organisation, e.g. the board of directors of a company

board of directors: group of directors elected by the shareholders to run a company

bookkeeper: person who keeps the financial records of a business

booming: expanding or becoming prosperous, e.g. business is booming

branch: local office of a bank or large business

brochure: publicity booklet

budget: plan of expected spending and income

capital expenditure: money spent on fixed assets (property, machines, furniture)

card: business card showing a person's name and the company he/she works for

carrier: company which transports goods

CEO: chief executive officer

CFO: chief financial officer

chain: a number of stores belonging to the same company, e.g. a chain of shoe shops, a hotel chain

Chamber of Commerce: group of local business people who meet to discuss problems which they have in common and to promote commerce in their town/area

chief: most important, e.g. chief accountant

chief executive officer: executive in charge of a company

CIF or c.i.f.: cost, insurance and freight (an export price that is given CIF includes the cost of transportation and insurance to the port of destination)

client: person or company with whom you do business or who pays for a service

club class: a class of airline ticket between first class and tourist

Co: company

colleague: person who works with you

commerce: business, the buying and selling of goods and services ('commercial' means related to business, e.g. commercial premises)

commission: money paid to a sales person or company, usually a percentage of the value of sales made

computer programmer: person who writes computer programs

computer software: computer programs (as opposed to computer hardware/machines)

consignment: 1 (informal use) a quantity of goods sent or to be sent
2 (technical use) goods sent to someone who then sells them for you in return for commission

construction company: company which specialises in building

consultant: specialist who gives advice

contact: person you know or person you can ask for help or advice

container: very large metal case for loading and transporting goods in trucks, trains and ships

contract: legal agreement between two parties

controller: person who controls, especially the finances of a company, e.g. financial controller

COO: chief operations officer

coordinator: person who organises the people and things involved in an activity, e.g. sales coordinator

cordless phone: phone that can be detached from its stand and thus be carried around within a certain distance from it

corporate hospitality: entertainment of important clients, usually by senior management

corporation: large company

cost-effective: producing the best results in relation to the cost incurred

costing: calculation of the costs and therefore the selling price of a product or service

credentials: written evidence giving proof of identity or authority

credit card: plastic card which allows you to borrow money and to buy goods without paying for them immediately – you pay the credit card company (e.g. Diners, Visa, Amex) later

credit control: checking that customers pay on time and do not owe more than their credit limit (credit controller is a person who checks payment and contacts customers when it is late)

credit note: note given to someone showing that an amount of money is owed to them

creditor: person or company to whom money is owed

courier: person or company that arranges to take parcels or messages from one place to another

customer service: department which deals with customers and their queries/complaints

Customs and Excise: UK government department which organises the collection of taxes on imports

data processing: analysing data stored in a computer in order to produce management information

degree: qualification obtained from a university, e.g. a degree in business studies

delegate: person who represents others at a meeting or conference

department: specialised section of a large company, e.g. sales department, department secretary

depot: central warehouse for goods, e.g. distribution depot

depressed: reduced; a 'depressed market' is one in which there are more goods than customers

deputy: person who can take the place of another, e.g. the deputy manager

despatch: send goods to a customer

devaluation: reduction in value of a currency against other currencies

digital projector: electronic equipment that projects from a laptop on to a screen

director: senior person who is in charge of a division or department, e.g. Personnel Director, Finance Director; senior directors are appointed by the shareholders

discount: percentage by which a full price is reduced (to a buyer) by the seller; 'volume discount' is a discount given to a customer who buys a large quantity of goods

distribution: sending goods from the manufacturer to the wholesaler and then to retailers

domestic: home, e.g. domestic market, domestic sales

door to door: 1 direct from one place to another
2 going from one house to the next, asking the occupiers to buy something or vote for someone

draft: first rough plan, e.g. draft schedule

E&OE: errors and omissions excepted (printed on an invoice to show that mistakes can be corrected at a later date)

engineer: person who looks after technical equipment, e.g. electrical engineer

estimate: calculation of probable cost or size or time of something

executive: usually a manager or director of a company who makes decisions (NB a 'sales executive' is a sales rep)

export: to sell goods to buyers in foreign countries

ex works: way of quoting a price which does not include transport from the factory, the price at the factory gate

factory floor: internal area of a factory where the manufacturing work is done

finance department: department which deals with the money used by a company

financial services: offering advice and financial products to consumers, e.g. pensions, savings plans

financial statement: document which shows the financial situation of a company

financial year: period, usually twelve months, used by companies for tax and accounting purposes

flexitime: system where workers can start or stop work at different hours provided that they work a certain number of hours per day or week

FOB or f.o.b.: free on board (price including all seller's costs until goods are on ship for transportation)

forwarder: person or company which arranges shipment of goods to their destination

forwarding agent: see forwarder

fund: money set aside for a special purpose; a 'fund management company' is a company that deals with the investment of sums of money on behalf of clients

GNP: a gross national product (value of goods and services produced in a country in a year, including income from other countries)

goods: products

gross figure: total figure with no deductions

group: several companies linked together in the same organisation, e.g. the group headquarters

guarantee: legal document which promises that a machine will work properly or that an item is of good quality

haulage company: company which transports goods by road

haulier: haulage company or person involved in the haulage business

hazpack certificated: certified to handle dangerous loads (often required of transportation companies)

head office: main office, where the board of directors works and meets

headed notepaper: notepaper with the name and address of a company printed on it

heavy manufacturing: making of large products, e.g. steel bars, ships, railway engines

hi-tech industries: industries using the most modern and sophisticated technology

home: in the country where a company is based, e.g. home market, home sales

human resources department: personnel department

import: goods bought from foreign suppliers and brought into a country

Inc. (US): incorporated

industrial estate: area specifically reserved for factories and warehouses

industrial park: industrial estate

industrial relations: relations between management and workers

insurance broker: person who arranges insurance for clients

interim: coming before the final version, e.g. interim results, interim payments

invest: 1 spend money on something which you believe will be useful, e.g. to invest money in new machinery, to invest in a factory
2 put money into shares, bonds etc. in the hope that it will produce interest and increase in value

investment: 1 purchase of machines, materials etc. in order to make goods to sell
2 placing of money so that it will produce interest and increase in value

invoice: (noun) note asking for payment for goods or services supplied
(verb) to send an invoice to someone

IT: information technology

itinerary: list of places to be visited on a journey or trip

labour: workforce

land line: a telephone that uses telephone lines (wires)

lease: to let or rent land, offices or machinery for a period of time

ledger: book or system in which accounts are kept

liaison officer: person responsible for communication and contact between organisations

limited company: company where members/shareholders are responsible for the debts only up to the value of the shares they hold

load: (noun) a volume of goods that are transported, e.g. a lorry load, a container load
(verb) to put goods into a transporter, e.g. to load a ship, to load goods onto a plane

loan: something which has been lent, usually money, e.g. bank loan

Ltd: limited, e.g. Joe Smith Ltd (see limited company)

logistics management: controlling the movement of goods; note also 'supply chain management'

machine hall: part of a factory where machines operate

mail order: system of buying and selling from a catalogue and delivering by mail

maintenance: keeping things going or working, e.g. maintenance department, maintenance engineer

management information system: equipment and procedures which provide managers with information, usually computerised

manager: head of a department in a company, e.g. transport manager, regional manager

managing director: director who is in charge of a whole company

manufacturer: person or company which produces machine-made products

margin: difference between the cost of a product and the money received with selling it, e.g. profit margin

market: area where a product might be sold, or group of people who might buy a product

marketing department: department in a company which specialises in using marketing techniques (e.g. packaging, advertising) to sell a product

MD: managing director

merchandise: goods which are for sale or have been sold

merchant: person who buys and sells goods in bulk for re-sale

merger: joining together of two or more companies

multinational (company): company which has branches or subsidiary companies in several countries

multiple retailer: chain of stores belonging to the same company

negotiable: 1 can be exchanged for cash, goods etc.
2 can be changed or agreed by discussion

net: price or weight or pay etc. after all deductions have been made

network: system that links different points together, e.g. a distribution network; a computer network

office manager: person responsible for the administration of an office or group of offices

office services: variety of services offered to an office, e.g. cleaning and maintenance, office equipment, service and repair

officer: title sometimes given to a person with an official position in a company, e.g. liaison officer

OHP: overhead projector

open plan office: large room divided into smaller working spaces with no fixed divisions between them

operation: business organisation and work, e.g. a company's operation in Eastern Europe

organisation chart: chart showing the way a company is organised, the names of the departments and the senior management

outlet: place where something can be sold

overdraft: money in excess of the amount in their account which a person or company can withdraw with the permission of the bank

overheads: costs not directly related to producing goods/services, e.g. directors' salaries

PA: personal assistant

packaging: materials used to protect goods which are being packed

pallet: flat wooden base on which goods can be stacked for easy handling by a forklift truck

paperwork: office work, especially writing memos and filling in forms

parent company: company which owns and controls a smaller company

partnership: unregistered business where two or more people (but not more than 20) share the risks and profits according to a partnership agreement

payroll: 1 list of people employed and paid by a company
2 money paid by a company in salaries

pension fund: money which provides pensions for retired members of staff

permanent staff: employees with a permanent contract, as opposed to temporary staff

personal assistant: secretary who works for one particular person

personnel: the people employed in an organisation

personnel department: section of a company which deals with staff matters (see also human resources department)

plant: factory

PLC: public limited company (see below)

power station: place where electricity is generated

pp: *per procreationem* (Latin); to pp a letter is to sign on behalf of someone else

PR: public relations

premises: building and the land it stands on

private sector: all companies which are owned by private shareholders, not by the site

processing plant: factory where raw materials are changed into products by the use of machinery

product: thing which is made or manufactured

production: making or manufacturing goods for sale

production planner: person who plans a production schedule

profile: brief description

profit and loss statement: statement of a company's expenditure and income over a period of time (almost always one calendar year) showing whether a company has made a profit or loss

progress report: report on how work is going

projected: planned or expected, e.g. projected figures

public limited company: company in which the general public can invest, and whose shares are bought and sold on the Stock Exchange

public relations: keeping good relations between a company and the general public

publicity material: sheets or posters or leaflets used to attract the attention of the public to products or services

purchaser: person or company which buys/purchases

purchasing department: department responsible for buying/purchasing

quality assurance: ensuring/checking that goods are of a certain standard

quote: quotation, an estimate of how much something will cost

R&D: Research and Development

range: series of items from which the customer can choose, e.g. *We offer a wide range of sizes*

rationalisation: process of streamlining or making more efficient

reception: place (in a hotel or office) where visitors register or say who they have come to see

recession: fall in trade or the economy

reclaim: claim back, e.g. reclaim travel expenses

recruitment agency: agency responsible for finding new staff for a company

redevelopment: rebuilding and/or modernising structures or facilities, e.g. factories, road systems

redundant: no longer employed, because the job is no longer necessary

refinery: factory where raw materials are processed to remove impurities, e.g. oil refinery, sugar refinery

refund: money paid back, e.g. for returned goods

registration number: official number, e.g. car registration number

remittance: money sent as payment for something

rep: representative, e.g. sales rep

representative: person or company which acts on another's behalf showing or selling goods or services

Research and Development department: department which carries out scientific investigation leading to new products or improvement of existing ones

retail: sale of general goods to the public, e.g. retail dealer, retail outlet

run: manage or organise

sales: 1 money received for selling something 2 number of items sold

sales conference: meeting of sales managers, representatives, publicity staff etc., to discuss results and future sales plans

schedule: timetable or plan made in advance

security: 1 staff who protect an office or factory, e.g. from burglars 2 system which protects, e.g. electronic security system

senior: older or more important, e.g. senior administrative manager

serial number: number in a series, used to identify a product

share: official document showing that the holder shares ownership of a company; shares usually entitle the holder to receive a dividend (share of the profits) and to vote at the AGM (Annual General Meeting)

shareholder: person who owns shares in a company

shift system: a system where one group of workers work for a period and are then replaced by another group

shipment: goods sent

shipping agent: company which specialises in the sending of goods

site: place or location, e.g. building site, factory site, site plan

skilled: having learnt certain skills, e.g. skilled worker

statement: detailed list; a 'financial statement' is a statement about financial position; a 'statement of expenses' is a detailed list of money spent

Stock Exchange: place where shares in public companies can be bought and sold

stocktaking: counting of goods in stock at the end of an accounting period

storage: keeping in a store or in a warehouse

store: storeroom, place where goods are kept

subcontract: to agree with a company that it will do part of the work for a project

subsidiary: company which is owned by a parent company

supervisor: person who organises work and checks that it is well done, e.g. production supervisor

supplier: person or company that supplies or sells goods or services

switchboard: central point in a telephone system, where all lines meet

systems analysis: person who specialises in systems analysis

takeover: buying a controlling interest in a business by buying more than 50% of its shares

target: goal to aim for, e.g. sales target

technician: person with technical expertise, e.g. electrical technician, laboratory technician

telecommunications: systems of passing messages over long distances, e.g. by cable, radio or satellite

telesales: sales made over the telephone

terms and conditions: conditions which have to be carried out as part of a contract, or arrangements which have to be agreed before a contract is valid

trade: wholesale, e.g. trade price, trade discount

trainee: person who is learning how to do something

turnover: total sales of a company including goods and services

union: organisation which represents its members in discussions with management, e.g. over wages and conditions of work

unit: single building or small department, e.g. medical unit, translation unit

upgrade: to increase the importance or quality of something, e.g. to upgrade a person's job, to upgrade from tourist to business class

VAT: value-added tax (UK sales tax)

vice president (US): one of the executive directors of a company

videophone: telephone which allows callers to see one another on a screen

voicemail: telephone system with recorded instructions to the user, which allows him/her to send or receive messages to be retrieved at a later time

voucher: paper which is given instead of money, e.g. lunch voucher

warehouse: large building where goods are stored

wholesale: buying goods in bulk from manufacturers and selling to retailers

workforce: all the workers in an office or factory

work in progress: goods which are partly manufactured or unfinished

works: factory, e.g. glass works, works manager

workshop: 1 small factory 2 area in a building where mechanical work is done